NOVEL VS. FICTION:
THE CONTEMPORARY REFORMATION

NOVEL VS. FICTION:
THE CONTEMPORARY REFORMATION

Edited by Jackson I. Cope
and Geoffrey Green

Pilgrim Books, Inc., Norman, Oklahoma

813
N85
139329
July 1986

Published in the United States by Pilgrim Books, Inc., P.O. Box 2399, Norman, OK 73070-2399

1981

ISBN 0-937664-56-1

CONTENTS

NOVEL VS. FICTION: THE CONTEMPORARY REFORMATION
Edited by Jackson I. Cope and Geoffrey Green

Introduction:
The Contemporary Reformation   1
    JACKSON I. COPE

Eximplosions   9
    CHRISTINE BROOKE-ROSE

What Are Experimental Novels and Why Are
    There So Many Left Unread?   23
    RAYMOND FEDERMAN

Relativism and the Multiple Contexts for
    Contemporary Fiction   33
    GEOFFREY GREEN

Robert Coover on His Own and Other Fictions   45
    ROBERT COOVER/LARRY McCAFFREY

Daniel Martin and the Mimetic Task   65
    ROBERT ALTER

Notes on the Novel-as-Autobiography   79
    PETER BAILEY

Barth, *Letters* and the Great Tradition   95
    MAX F. SCHULZ

Comic Structure and the Double Time-Scheme
    of Hawkes's *Second Skin*   117
    DONALD R. WINEKE

Reestablishing Innocence: A Conversation
  with Leslie Fiedler   133
    LESLIE FIEDLER/ GEOFFREY GREEN

Generic Geographies   151
    JACKSON I. COPE

NOVEL VS. FICTION:
THE CONTEMPORARY REFORMATION

Introduction: The Contemporary Reformation

Jackson I. Cope
University of Southern California

Most of my critical thinking, public and private, has been given to literature of the Renaissance, the era most obviously associated with the birth and proliferation of genres as widespread phenomena in critical discourse. Even so, throughout my career I have maintained an uneasy uncertainty as to whether genres existed, or where, if at all. My interests in the Renaissance, however—and especially in the critical discourses of the Renaissance—have led me to modern and contemporary literature and the critical discourses of our time. When I was approached about the possibility of this volume, I was writing about the fiction of Robert Coover, trying to understand the nature of its innovativeness and the sources of excitement with which it had renewed my general critical alertness. In discussion of these matters with a new friend and colleague, Geoffrey Green, fiction writer and critic, we concluded that we might identify good writers of experimental fiction willing to talk about their own work and that of others. Thereafter, we gathered the essays of this collection devoted to a fiction being written in our time which departs from the rough but nonetheless clearly understood contours of the novel. For me it has been an experience of gradually clarifying, without laying to rest, puzzlements—puzzlements sharpened by my critical imagination's division (one always hopes for an element of fusion) between our own literature and that of the Renaissance.

First, a few thoughts about the Renaissance. In the century and a half, more or less, which that tag conveys to literary historians, there emerged a never-equalled body of creativity in epic and dramatic forms. On the other hand, the novella, the fictional prose narrative, had been familiar from the Middle Ages but did not develop at all significantly in its Renaissance phase until the late exception of the *Quijote*, which only much later would become a touchstone and model for another form which Cervantes had no notion he was shaping when he began: the novel. Why was this so? Why was the *Decameron* aped and not equalled by its myriad emulators in the following centuries? why did the *Quijote* not spawn a myriad novelists in the later Renaissance? Why so, when epic and drama were achieving a creative richness unequalled before or after?

The answer, of course, is obvious, but obviously leads us into some paradoxical truths about a strange symbiosis which bears upon the state of contemporary fiction. Donatus had told the Middle Ages so little about tragedy and comedy in such definitive fashion that he offered no potential playwright either guidance or goad. But the recovery of Aristotle's poetic into a rather wide public domain in the sixteenth century, the observations upon the *Poetics* interpreted and expanded into thousands of pages by dozens of (mainly Italian) critics occurred simultaneously with the birth and highest pitch of modern drama. The Renaissance was, in Baxter Hathaway's happy phrase, an Age of Criticism. That truism leads, of course, to a paradox because this criticism was highly prescriptive, in fact if not intention, yet none of the English dramatists we anthologize—Marlowe, Marston, Middleton, et al—seem to have filled its prescriptions. Clearly, the evidence leads to the pragmatic probability that critical theory, generic theory pursued to the veriest details, was necessary to the creation of a major dramatic literature. Yet the body of drama produced conformed so little to the critics' generic rulings that one is hardput to find an enduring play which Castelvetro or Campanella would have accepted as a true exemplar of either tragedy or comedy. Finally, Guarini, having written *Il pastor fido*, turned this absurd situation on its head and wrote a critical tract describing "tragicommedia," a new genre of which his own play was the only extant example. Or turn to epic. Petrarca slept with his Homer, but the *Africa* is an ignored history in hexameters, not a Homeric epic. But with the recovery of generic theory in the *Poetics*, the Renaissance immediately began to emulate and to challenge its literary heritage, creating not only the generic debate about epic and romance which focused upon Ariosto, but also generating the modern epic in

Tasso and Milton. Shakespeare, some think, wrote a bit into *Hamlet* about the Aristotelian protagonist, larger in place and posture than ourselves but flawed by "that vicious mole of nature" which devours the general good. But in any case Shakespeare would have found it difficult *not* to know the tendency of the *Poetics* on tragedy. Yet what might Aristotle (had he been as prescriptive as many Renaissance epigoni made him seem) have made of Lear: an old, fatuous, irascible ego at the beginning of the play of which he is protagonist? Aristotle turned upside-down as Shakespeare leads us through Lear's heath of soul-making, as if he conceived a generic challenge to create an anti-Oedipus, one who gains his eyes at the last?

These are examples, even a paradigm offered by the Renaissance toward understanding the contemporary reformation of the novel. What we discover is an unmistakable symbiosis between an assertive body of critical theory, generic definition and prescription, and the enrichment writers receive from it as both validation and challenge to the enterprise of turning fantasy into new forms of fiction.[1]

> Standing at the confluence of so many literary traditions and genres, Joyce's *Ulysses* has become the supreme challenge for the theoretical critic of fiction. . . . we cannot begin to perceive without a framework of illusions, of provisional hypotheses, and in the case of *Ulysses* these hypotheses are provided by our experience of the genres. . . . *Ulysses* lives in our minds as both process and product, . . . and any theory which threatens this double sense, whether it be put forward in the cause of the "novel" or some other genre, is ultimately self-defeating.[2]

Wise words by Walton Litz which focus the history of twentieth-century fiction upon that great touchstone of demarcation between a genre produced by the Victorians and in process of dissolution, reformation by ourselves. Boccaccio's followers in the *novella* form could not develop in the same creative way as dramatists and epic poets could in the Renaissance because the novelistic "genre" did not exist as a body of critical description; it confronted the dramatist Cervantes and later the dramatist Fielding as a sub-literature, a formlessness without either the authority or the arbitrariness of a known past. Happily, of course, this situation was changed by the gradual probing after forms for exploring society and psyche upon which we and Joyce were teethed, the "novel" of the past two centuries. And always in the formulation of this form there must have been a restlessness about paradoxes. I cite the OED: "Genre: kind, sort, style. A style of painting which depicts scenes and

subjects of common life." How well this conception dovetails with the
entry for "novel": "a fictitious prose narrative of considerable length, in
which characters and actions representative of real life are portrayed in a
plot of more or less complexity." But how oddly that "generic" usage
fails to fit with the primary definition of "novel": "something new; a
novelty; News." And it is just here that my puzzlement about the direction of recent fiction begins to merge with my puzzlement about the
relationship of criticism to creativity in the Renaissance. What do rep-
resentations of real life of considerable length have to do with novelty,
news? On the evening news we get vignettes, oddities and novelties of
the moment, but real life and the novel are of considerable length, and
lives liken as they lengthen and there is no one new under the sun. Indeed, has not just that been the appeal of the novel perenially in its
largest mass for the largest masses? Unlike the tragic protagonist, the
novelistic protagonist has been characteristically *only* ordinary, life-
sized, Emma Bovary to Augie March, explorers within a field of interaction between a mere self and massive society.

Society, of course, took its most recently dominant metaphor from
self in that chronological confluence which saw the coming to maturity
of Darwinism, Marxism, and of the novel as mass entertainment and
education. It seems inevitable, therefore, that the eminent Victorian
theoretician David Masson should have set out early upon the enterprise of discriminating among his more creative contemporaries in the
writing of fiction ("the novelist, as the creator of his mimic world, is
also its providence; he makes the laws that govern it"), but did so only
to conclude that "it is possible then to see how far his laws of moral
government are in accordance with those that rule the real course of
things, and so, on the one hand, how deeply and with what accuracy he
has studied life, and, on the other, whether after his study he is a loyal
member of the human commonwealth, or a rebel, a cynic, a son of the
wilderness."[3] The novelist presented as a pseudo-deity, then, only provisionally free to either mimic the normative values of real life or to
wander in fallen exile.

It is a surprisingly short leap from this Victorian critical dictum to
an important aspect of neo-Marxist theory of the novel as articulated by
its most sophisticated exponent in our own time, Georg Lukács. Let
me cite a few passages which recouch the moral determinism of Masson
in contemporary phraseology, although displacing the emphasis of the
nineteenth-century critic from the obligatory debt of the author to society onto that supposedly owed by the character he creates:

It is not a particular condition of society or, at least, it is only apparently a condition which is portrayed. The most important thing is to show how the *direction* of a social tendency becomes visible in the small, imperceptible capillary movements of individual life.

To fulfill the aims of the novel all that is required is to show convincingly and powerfully the irresistible course of social-historical development. The essential aim of the novel is the representation of the ways society moves. . . .

Therefore the general historicity . . . of drama, does not suffice for the novel. It must be historically authentic in root and branch.[4]

"Root and branch"; "society moves"; "the imperceptible capillary movements of individual life"—these are Lukács' metaphors spawned by a Darwinian world upon the novel, making that genre, as it had made society, mirror of an organism with its own chronological and individuating structure and growth. Or, structure as growth.[5]

The flourishing of the Renaissance; the flowering of New England: always we turn instinctively to these organic metaphors of growth, of an arc of development to its natural beauty after which culmination the productions generated by, generic to a period dry upon the stem, entombed through the same temporal process by which they were brought forth from the womb of time. It is something we sense as critical botanists (the first botanist Theophrastus being Aristotle's successor), this urge to encompass movement by immobilizing its form under the microscope of definition. And there, as in all classifications of the generational process, we find not the flower but its inwardness paradoxically dried into the bare bones of a skeleton. And of a dinosaur, at that, if we shift the metaphor to suit our relationship to the novelistic genre. For there is little organic, in any case, in a contemporary universe intent upon the extension of old modes by mechanical and electronic means, and the deconstruction of old genres into non-texts which sometimes seem as playfully fluid and unpredictable as random experiment.

But let me tell you a story, a modern instance, about a baby-sitter and a matron who both got into trouble. The sitter arrives at the Tuckers' residence at 7:40 to feed, bathe and put to bed their two children and an infant while the parents attend a party. The television is blaring; the children are rebellious; Mrs. Tucker is disappointed with life and pinched into her girdle to the point of worry about blood circulation and heart failure. The sitter's boyfriend Jack wonders about dropping by in the hope of a sexual initiation on the Tuckers' sofa; he broaches the notion to his friend Mark as they play a pinball machine. Mr. Tucker thinks about how the sitter had used their tub the last time, fantasizes about catching her soaking there should he return unexpectedly while she was watching television and necking with some kid on the sofa. The children tickle, wrestle, then spank the sitter while Jack and Mark peer in the window as she and Mr. Tucker leap from the tub in which he has joined her only to brain himself on the washstand. While Mr. Tucker has left the party to peer into the window to watch his child-son spanking the sitter, his wife is being buttered and then tugged at by the remaining guests to get her back into the girdle she had lowered in the bathroom while the boy, as punishment for wetting his pants, has to get into the tub with the sitter. Mark is kissing her while Jack's inexperienced hands tentatively remove the sitter's flimsy panties beneath the blanket as she realizes it is, at last, going to happen. The sheriff on the TV western smashes the dark-jawed villain as the boy calls to the sitter that the baby in the tub is not moving or swimming or anything. Jack smashes Mark in the jaw when Mark has bruised the sobbing sitter and torn her skirt; this at 8:30 when Mr. Tucker returns to the house, drink in hand, to catch Jack and the sitter, to chase the boy out "bareassed" and lower himself onto the sofa with the naked, nubile girl who he found just stepping into the tub where he joined her at 8:00 when, sirens wailing, his wife, the entire group of party-goers, and the police found them: "Dolly! My God, Dolly, I can explain!" She glowers down at them, ripped girdle around her ankles, and replies, " What the four of you are doing in the bathtub with *my* babysitter?"

The rape, the children's sex play, the seduction, the deaths by accident, murder, the television shows interact in a rising crescendo of incompatibilities until the baby-sitter hears the report of her own death on the evening news program; until, in the end, after all this channel switching, back at the original party:

> "What can I say, Dolly?" the host says with a sigh. . . . "Your children are murdered, your husband gone, a corpse in your bathtub, and your house is wrecked. I'm sorry. But what can I say?" On the TV the news is over, and they're selling aspirin. "Well, I don't know," she says. "Let's see what's on the late late movie."[6]

Half a dozen incompatible story lines and endings are given validation by fiat in Robert Coover's widely-reprinted story, "The Baby-Sitter." Throughout the fiction the interweaving of romance and violence as they are projected by the television and acted out suggest a real problem of contemporary concern, an affinity with those "characters and actions representative of real life" of which the OED spoke in defining the novel. But the interaction challenges any mimetic or organicist theory: no organism grows in multiple mutually-exclusive directions simultaneously. This is a not uncharacteristic exemplar of a recognizable body of contemporary fiction. The work of Barth and Barthelme, of Calvino and Coover, of Federman and Fiedler, of Gass and Hawkes, and of that discouragingly large group I have not read, but have read of—these are works with a discipline manifestly equal to that exercised upon the most satisfying "novels." One might even say that they are equal to, often superior to the earlier novel in their adherence to "real life." But the real life forms echoed in "The Baby-Sitter" are those which structure the fantasy. We are accustomed to speaking of the mythic novel since the appearance of *Ulysses*, that great touchstone of whose generic importance Walton Litz reminds us. But with the fairy tale adapted so often in Coover's fiction, adapted most notoriously in Barthelme's *Snow White*; with the folktale adapted into a veritable anthology in Garcia Márquez' *One Hundred Years of Solitude*; with the detective story adapted to new purposes in Manuel Puig's *Buenos Aires Affair*—in such exemplars we are brought back to the important truism that myth is attractive to the literate fantasy because it has so strict and limited a structure that it can be recognized as inevitable form even in the most unanticipated recombinations, cross-breedings. But so viewed, myth is only another view of genre, perimeter of the human fantasy's shuttle between freedom and limitation. As in a kaleidoscope, the contemporary writer has sensed the combinations to be infinitely teasing in their possibilities, but severely limited in the pieces with which we play. On the Tuckers' television set, the baby-sitter is presented with a sadistic battle of strength as Black Bart tries to rape the schoolmarm and the sheriff saves her from a fate which in fantasy and the myth which it projects is worse than death. She is also presented with the ethereal swirlings of adolescent fantasia, at the other extreme of simplicity, in one of those innumerable musical comedies of the forties and forever ("they whirl aerily, stirring a light breeze, through a magical landscape of rose and emerald. . . . He smiles in a pulsing crescendo of sincerity and song"). But the real life of Coover's fantasy and of the baby-sitter's is no more complicated than these projections except in the crucial fact of recognition and in the fictional recombinings which make these plays of fantasy also epiphanies of the playground within. The working out becomes simultaneously a show of how it works.

I do not begin to understand much of what is happening through fiction today, but I suppose no one really does. And the Renaissance is easier to survey through the telescope of time past, so it helps me sense that the presence of a large and aggressive body of criticism has been necessary to stimulate a creative reaction. That reaction has been a swing of the needle across a spectrum of realism which runs from "a social tendency become visible in the small, imperceptible capillary movements of individual life" back to play with and upon the lack of individuation inherent in the mythic fantasy. If, as I suggest, myth is really an enveloping analogue to the literary notion of genre, then it has worked to use the more particular genre of novel against itself in the creation of our fiction. It is more than rhetorical to suggest that this fiction constitutes a new "realism."

NOTES

1. Rosalie Colie, *The Resources of Kind: Genre-Theory in the Renaissance,* ed. B. K. Lewalski (Berkeley, 1973) argues the case for a proliferation of genres and generic interaction in the various categories *she* must invent for Renaissance innovations (*genera mista, nova reperta,* inclusionism). The proliferation itself serves to underline the dominant Aristotelian modes as continuing models to be emulated and tinkered with toward "the *literary* gain . . . both in having genres and in refusing to allow generic categories to dictate or predestine the size, scope, content, and manner in any particular literary work" (p. 103).

2. A. Walton Litz, "The Genre of 'Ulysses,' " in *The Theory of the Novel: New Essays,* ed. John Halperin (Oxford Univ. Press, 1974), pp. 109, 119, 120.

3. *British Novelists and Their Styles* (1859), p. 23, cited by John Halperin, "The Theory of the Novel: A Critical Introduction," in *Theory of the Novel,* p. 9.

4. Georg Lukács, *The Historical Novel,* trans. Hannah and Stanley Mitchell (1937; New Jersey, 1978), pp. 144, 144, 151.

5. Alastair Fowler, "The Life and Death of Literary Forms," *NLH,* 2 (1971), 199–216 offers a discussion of the pertinency and sophistications of the organic metaphor in contention with René Wellek.

6. Robert Coover, *Pricksongs & Descants: Fictions* (New York, 1969), p. 239.

Eximplosions

Christine Brooke-Rose
Université de Paris VIII

i. *Silence and the limits of consciousness*

Towards the end of a landmark essay, "The Aesthetics of Silence" (1966), Susan Sontag wrote:

> art, in the modern conception, is always connected with systematic transgressions of a formal sort. The systematic violation of older formal conventions practiced by modern artists gives their work a certain aura of the unspeakable—for instance, as the audience uneasily senses the negative presence of what else could be, but isn't being, said; and as any "statement" made in an aggressively new or difficult form tends to seem equivocal or merely vacant. (p. 31)[1]

These features, however, "must not be acknowledged at the expense of one's awareness of the positivity of the work of art," and she ends the section with this crucial paragraph:

> For instance, each work of art gives us a form or paradigm or model of *knowing* something, an epistemology. But viewed as a spiritual project . . . , what any work of art supplies is a specific model for meta-social or meta-ethical *tact*, a standard of decorum. Each artwork indicates the unity of certain preferences about what can and cannot be said (represented). At the same time that it may make a tacit proposal for upsetting previously consecrated rulings on what can be said (or represented), it issues its own set of limits. (pp. 31–32)

It may seem odd to speak of "decorum"—that ultra-classical concept—in a context of an art that most critics describe in more explosive terms. But Sontag is right, not only in emphasizing the limits of any new art form, but also in distinguishing, as she does a moment later, between two styles, loud and soft, in which contemporary artists advocate silence.

The loud style, which tends to be frenetic and over-generalizing, is a

9

function of the unstable antithesis of plenum and void. It is often apocalyptic and must endure the indignity of all apocalyptic thinking, that
of outliving the prophesied end and setting "a new date for the inciner-
ation of consciousness and the definitive pollution of language and exhaustion of the possibilities of art-discourse" (p. 31). The soft style is
more cautious, and basically "an extension of traditional classicism: the
concern with modes of propriety, with standards of seemliness. Silence
is only 'reticence' stepped up to the nth degree," though of course "in
the translation of this concern from the matrix of traditional classical
art, the tone has changed—from didactic seriousness to ironic open-
mindedness" (p. 31). But its advocates (such as John Cage, Jasper
Johns) "are reacting to the same absolute aspirations (by programmatic
disavowals of art); they share the same disdain for 'meanings' established by bourgeois-rationalist culture, indeed for culture itself in the
familiar sense. What is voiced by the Futurists, some of the Dada artists, and Burroughs as a harsh despair and perverse vision of apocalypse
is no less serious for being proclaimed in a polite voice and as a sequence of playful affirmations" (p. 32).

One might say in fact that the "unstable antithesis of plenum and
void" is itself at the basis of that other antithesis of loud and soft,
which Sontag expresses more frequently as paradox: "The art of our
time is noisy with appeals for silence" (p. 12): "The tendency is towards
less and less. But never has 'less' so ostentatiously advanced itself as
'more' " (p. 14); "in the era of the widespread advocacy of art's silence,
an increasing number of works babble. Verbosity and repetitiveness are
particularly noticeable in the temporal arts of prose fiction, music, film
and dance . . . " (pp. 26–27).

It is true that art is suffering from an acute consciousness of plenum
and void, that it is "foundering on the debilitating tide of what once
seemed the crowning achievement of European thought: secular historical consciousness. In little more than two centuries, the consciousness
of history had transformed itself from a liberation . . . into an almost
insupportable burden of self-consciousness. It's scarcely possible for the
artist to write a word (or render an image or make a gesture) that
doesn't remind him of something already achieved" (p. 14). Language
is experienced as fallen, corrupt, weighed down by historical accumula-
tion (p. 15).

Hence the dream of a wholly ahistorical and therefore unalienated
art, and silence (not literal of course, except in artistic or real suicides

like Rimbaud's, Lautréamont's, Mayakovsky, etc.), as a metaphor for a cleansed, non-interfering vision. Traditional art invites the *look*—mobile, voluntary, varying in intensity. Modern art invites the *stare*—steady, unmodulated, fixed, with its character of compulsion, unsolicited but allowing no realease from attention (p. 15). Art should be approached like a landscape, which demands no understanding, no imputations of significance, no investment of anxieties or sympathies, but rather, the spectator's absence; "it asks that he not add anything to *it*." A contemplation, which means self-forgetfulness:

> Toward such an ideal plenitude to which the audience can add nothing, analogous to the aesthetic relation to nature, a great deal of contemporary art aspires—through various strategies of blandness, of reduction, of deindividuation, of alogicality. In principle, the audience may not even add its thought. All objects, rightly perceived, are already full. This is what Cage must mean when, after explaining that there is no such thing as silence because something is always happening that makes a sound, he adds, "No one can have an idea once he starts really listening." (p. 16)

This, we may note, is in absolute contradiction with Barthes' now more fashionable notion of "writerly" text, in which the reader participates actively, as well as with all the more recent critical activity on the reader, the latter, however, chiefly concerned with more traditional texts. For Barthes, though, it is precisely the modern text which is *scriptible*. Similarly "plenitude," in the sense of obsessive information-giving, is regarded by Barthes as a mark of the classic text, the "readerly," which the reader passively absorbs. And Sontag appears to contradict herself in the very next paragraph when she says that "plenitude—experiencing all the space as filled, so that ideas cannot enter—means impenetrability. A person who becomes silent becomes opaque for the other; somebody's silence opens up an array of possibilities for interpreting that silence, for imputing speech to it" (p. 16). And again later when, considering the various uses of silence, one of them is said to be to "keep things open," for "speech closes off thought (An example: the enterprise of criticism, in which there seems no way for a critic not to assert that a given artist is *this*, he's *that*, etc.)" (pp. 19–20).

We may perhaps fruitfully contrast this possible contradiction (or paradox) with Julia Kristeva's view of modern literature as that which (more or less) consciously sets out to enlarge the limits of the human signifiable, as opposed to the media whose function is to collectivize the systems of signs and even the unconscious.[2] Modern "experience-of-limits" writing singularizes, and goes very far into the mechanisms that constitute human consciousness, even to the obscure mechanism of so-called primary narcissism, where the subject constitutes himself—insofar as he opposes—into another (psychosis). In this sense it takes over from psychoanalysis and is its strangest rival, psychoanalysis having itself taken the place of a certain kind of literary fantasy. This was, incidentally, one of the reasons for which Todorov placed the fantastic in a limited period, its "themes" having become the privileged domain of psychoanalysis.

According to Kristeva, then, modern literature of the "experience of limits" would have recaptured this domain. With Artaud, Bataille, Burroughs, she says, writing seems to have a more direct access to the asymbolic proper to psychosis, through the logical and phonetic drift which pulverizes and multiplies meaning, pretending to play with it or to flee it in order the better to endure it, or through the cut-up of Burroughs unfolding and leaving in suspense the logic of the narrative and of the speaking subject. And she compares this exploration of the imaginative area to the relation with the mother, to the pre-sign, as for example in the theater of gesture, sound, color, rhythm (Cage, Bob Wilson). Writing is a technique of the imaginary, of the *fantasme* (fantasy in the psychological sense), but has always simulated, mimed, what is communal in this fantasy. With the experience of limits, that imaginary is led to a point where it leaves the community. "It fixes in signs what, in the imagination, is irreducible to the experience of others, what is most singular, even if no one escapes that singularity." In fact "we confront idiolects, which proliferate, uncontrollable, and the only risk (huge) is that they will remain solitary, invisible monuments in a society that tends on the contrary to uniformisation."[3] The one-time fantasmatic *camera obscura* (such as the characters of nineteenth-century fiction) has become a brilliant television screen, and writing has now ventured out as reconnaissance-scout to the limits of the unnameable, "distrusting the unconscious as bestseller, fantasy for all, warned by the experience of the twentieth century that by generalising fantasy one reaches the most massive, that of the extermination camp. . . . Never before has this exploration of the limits of meaning been attempted in such an unprotected manner, that is, without religious, mystical or other justification."

These are large claims, though Susan Sontag is perhaps more cautious, more aware of contradictions and of limitations. And other large claims have been made for "postmodernism," notably by Ihab Hassan. But first, we should perhaps clarify the notion: what exactly is "postmodernism," if we must use that term, and who represents it?

ii. "Postmodernism"—what is it?

Susan Sontag mentions few novelists, though when she talks of the emptying out of consciousness as prerequisite to the ability to perceive what one is "full of," what words and mechanized gestures one is stuffed with, she contrasts Rilke's and Ponge's "benign nominalism" with the more brutal nominalism found in the aesthetics of the inventory, of dehumanization and impersonalization (Roussel, early Warhol films, early Robbe-Grillet). And when she discusses the ambivalent attitude to language (a high estimate of its powers and past health against an awareness of its current dangers), she notes that this leads to an impulse towards a discourse that "appears both irrepressible (and in principle interminable), and strangely inarticulate, painfully reduced," giving Gertrude Stein, Burroughs and Beckett as examples of "the subliminal idea that it might be possible to out-talk language, or to talk oneself into silence" (pp. 24–25, 27). She comments that this, though not a very promising strategy, is not so odd since the aesthetics of silence is often accompanied by "a barely controlled abhorrence of the void," and that "accommodating these two contrary impulses may produce the need to fill up all the spaces with objects of slight emotional weight or with areas of barely modulated color or evenly detailed objects, or to spin a discourse with as few possible inflections, emotive variations and risings and fallings of emphasis. These procedures seem analogous to the behavior of an obsessional neurotic warding off danger." She adds that the emotional fires feeding such a discourse may be turned down so low as to make it become a "steady hum or drone. What is left to the eye is a neat filling of a space with things, or, more accurately, the patient transcription of the surface detail of things" (pp. 27–28), and seems here to have Robbe-Grillet in mind (for objects, and, possibly, for emotive impulses, Nathalie Sarraute), although there is much more to their work than that, and, moreover, this "abhorrence of the void" and uninflected discourse are precisely what Barthes attributes to the nineteenth-century realist novel, but for ideological reasons and with consequent effects quite the opposite to those of Robbe-Grillet.

But Sontag is concerned with the general aesthetics of modern art, not with the detail of specific works, and the term "postmodernism" had not gained currency at the time of her still remarkable, elegant essay, in many ways a proleptic summary of much that has been said since. "Postmodernism" is now opposed to "Modernism" (Joyce, Pound, Eliot, Woolf, Stein, etc.) as not so much a falling off, but as something "new," more "Modern." But there seems to be a certain confusion as to just what it involves.

I find both terms peculiarly unimaginative for a criticism that purports to deal with phenomena of which the most striking feature is imagination, and I shall use them only when discussing critics who use them. For one thing, they are purely historical, period words, and in that sense traditional. In his stimulating but mimetically chaotic *Paracriticisms* (1975), Ihab Hassan at one point quotes eight critics (Ter Braak, Barthes, Blanchot, Starobinski, Poulet, Walter Benjamin, Morse Peckham and Frye) to show that their statements form a mosaic in which a certain movement can be discerned "away from the literalities of critics and away from its previous formal and historical definition . . . a movement beyond the control of the art object, toward the openness, and even the gratuitousness . . . of existence" (p. 27).

But what does he mean by "previous formal and historical definitions"? The very terms "modern" and "postmodern" (which he adopts) are historical, and as to formal definitions, surely any attempt, including his own, to discuss this particular explosion in art is bound to use some formal definitions, if only in the gathering together of the typical features of "modern" and "postmodern" art.

Secondly, they are self-cancelling terms, and this may be particularly apt for an art continually described as self-cancelling. But although criticism can thus be imbued with its objects, as Hassan brilliantly demonstrates with his constant counterpoints, re-visions, queries, digressions, other visions, and juxtaposing typography, I don't think that the labels should to that extent contain such built-in obsolescence. As C. S. Lewis said in quite another context: "Surely the analysis of water should not itself be wet?" For the labels are self-cancelling in an uncreative way. The Romantics used the term "modern art" until Schlegel popularized the term "romantic" as opposed to "antique" or "classical." Henry James used the term "the new novel." Our New Criticism, whatever its other qualities, hardly seems new today, nor does the *Nouvelle Critique* of the fifties. The French were obliged to use *nouveau nouveau roman* after the *nouveau roman*. I always preferred the term *anti-roman* for that particular phenomenon, which at least meant something (and in fact dates back to the sixteenth-century with Sorel's *Le Berger Extravagant*, subtitled *anti-roman*). Claude Mauriac spoke at the time of *alittérature* (1958), but neither of these caught on. "Postmodernism" is a sort of English equivalent to *nouveau nouveau*, for it merely means moderner modern, although it could in itself (and sometimes does) imply a reaction against "modernism."

These terms seem to me to be completely lacking in content, and the danger is that anyone may (and does) tend to put any content he likes into them, whereas traditional terms like—at random—symbolism, imagism, futurism, surrealism, did give some sort of orientation as to what was at stake.

Thirdly, and by way of corollary, the terms are simply lazy, inadequate. For fifty years or so we were content to call anything difficult of access modern art. In retrospect, much of it seems less or not at all difficult of access, so that the term "modern" is now used to cover any of the "great names" which have survived. But if we are going to put D. H. Lawrence (for eroticism and apocalyptism) and Hemingway and Proust and Kafka and Pound and Yeats and Eliot and Faulkner and Mann and Gide and Musil and Stevens and Virginia Woolf and Joyce, etc. into the same modernist ragbag, the term becomes meaningless except as a purely period term, itself obsolescent since modern by definition means now. Hassan admits privately that the term "postmodernism" is unsatisfactory, and in his book rightly insists on fluctuating frontiers, regarding Kafka as more postmodern than modern, and naturally points to antecedents such as Rabelais and Sterne; and in his 1978 MLA paper, he says that "we continually discover 'antecedents' of postmodernism—in Sterne, Sade, Blake, Lautréamont, Rimbaud, Jarry, Tzara, Hoffmannsthal, Gertrude Stein, the later Joyce, the later Pound, Duchamp, Artaud, Roussel, Broch, Queneau and Kafka. What this really means is that we have created in our mind a model of postmodernism, a particular typology of culture and imagination, and have proceeded to 'rediscover' the affinities of various authors and different moments with that model. We have, that is, reinvented our ancestors—and always shall."

This is aptly playful, but, as he himself implies in his "always shall," not very illuminating (the "moderns" rediscovered the Metaphysical Poets, the Romantics rediscovered the Middle Ages, the Classics rediscovered the Greeks and Romans, as did the Renaissance in other ways, etc.). And what is that model of "postmodernism"? How can one talk of a "model" if one rejects both historical and formal definitions? Hassan approvingly quotes Murray Krieger who asks, in *The Tragic Vision*: "how, if we limit ourselves to technical literary definitions, can we find for the tragic any meaning beyond that of Aristotle? The answer is, by moving from formalist aesthetics to what I would term 'thematics' " (Hassan, p. 7). The irony of that statement lies in the fact that "thematics," thus presented as a new idea, has long been considered (from the Russian Formalists right through to Post-Structuralist Deconstructivism) as the heavy death-mask of traditional criticism, to which, apparently, we are now urged to return.

In fact, of course, nothing is ever so ruthlessly to be rejected as *dépassé*, except in its manner and method. Both formal and thematic definitions are necessary, as are both subjective and objective approaches. But the dangers of all these and any others should be kept in mind, as well as the confusing effect of mixing them up without appearing to.

Paracriticisms is essentially a summary book rather than a critical one: like the works it deals with, it must be read, with its "dialogical" manner and its immense but lightly carried learning. It is a book full of "exits," rather like Barthes' codes, and reading it is in fact a little like reading later Barthes, *Le plaisir du texte*, for instance, in which one feels as if one were replunging into the intuitive and personal richness of the best New Criticism but after having been through the rigors of Structuralism, left behind by Barthes but somehow there in his tone and terminology. Hassan is more carefree (more slapdash at times), but the stimulus from both the learning and the provocative manner is felt.

iii. *Where do we go from here?*

Towards silence, exhaustion? Or a new beginning? A good "theory" (model) should be able to "predict," not in the futurological sense, but in accounting for all the theoretical possibilities. I am not a pure theorist, and even less a prophet, and critical prophecies have a way of being undone by artists. Apocalyptic prophets can be pessimistic (total destruction) or optimistic (death and renewal).

One absurd fallacy should perhaps be got out of the way: the "death of the novel" has been announced for half a century or more, and journalistic critics always mock this and point out that thousands of novels go on getting published and read, because people will always want "stories." That is entirely beside the point. Stories of one kind or another (even stories about stories) will indeed always continue, but they have always found and will continue to find their home in different forms. When the medieval verse romance got exhausted it became prose romance, and when that got exhausted, roughly in the fourteenth century, romances went on being written for at least a hundred years, and even well (Malory), just as Chaucer wrote an excellent verse romance (but in stanza form) a century after its heyday. But stories eventually found a more vivid form in the theater, which regalvanized story-telling later into epic, then satire and the novel. The great nineteenth-century novel has continued, in both diluted and revivified forms, right through the twentieth, but it has for a long time shown signs of exhaustion in its turn, so that stories have escaped into the new media, film and its younger, as yet babbling offspring, television. Hence the "elitist" wave of experiment and iconoclastic deconstructionism and stylization of various kinds. The wave itself, in its concern about non-interpretation and its self-reflexive ways of dealing with it, is a sign of decadence and apocalyptic premonitions, like the multiplication of rhetorics and their concern for systems of meaning.

It is true, however, that iconoclasm as such cannot last (I mean the individual works may last but not the deconstruction). As David Lodge says in a more specific context, "it would truly abolish itself, by destroying the norms against which we perceive its deviations."[4] Similarly, Susan Sontag:

> The present prospect is that artists will go on abolishing art, only to resurrect it in a more retracted version. As long as art bears up under the pressure of chronic interrogation, it would seem desirable that some of the questions have a certain playful quality.

But this prospect depends, perhaps, on the viability of irony itself. (p. 33)

I have postponed the problem of irony, and clearly I shall not solve it here. Barthes dismisses it as just another code that merely shows the superiority of one voice over another, which closes off the plurality of codes, and he insists that it has disappeared from modern writing, thanks to the degree zero of tone, already nascent (as *uncertainty* of irony) in Flaubert—for the idol must be disculpated.[5] Sontag also casts doubt on irony, for although it has been valued from Socrates on as a serious method of seeking and holding one's truth and saving one's sanity, "as it becomes the good taste of what is, after all, an essentially collective activity—the making of art—it may prove less serviceable" (p. 34). She adds that we need not judge it as categorically as Nietzsche, who equated the spread of irony throughout a culture with decadence and the approaching end of that culture's vitality, but "there still remains a question as to how far the resources of irony can be stretched. It seems unlikely that the possibilities of continually undermining one's assumptions can go on unfolding indefinitely into the future, without being checked by despair or by a laughter that leaves one without any breath at all" (p. 34). Similarly, Hassan talks of a self-consuming irony.

The writers in whom I am interested depend a great deal on irony, on more than a humdrum collusion with the reader (for collusion there must be). Some of the irony is naive, curiously mingled with earnestness and sometimes (if it is irony) astonishingly regressive in character, for instance in the treatment of sex, which is often ludicrously, limitedly, and it seems unconsciously phallocratic in many writers, with the exception of Barthelme and Brautigan. But the healthy signs are surely the very element of naivety I commented on, not by way of carping but to bring them out as such. If Frye is right, an exhausted literature turns to more popular forms, either directly, in the sense that they are themselves taken more seriously by the "central" tradition, or indirectly, in the sense of parody and stylization by the "serious" artists of that "central" tradition. The fact that this is happening so late, so long after the forms have become stereotypes, often parodied and even declared moribund, is one of the paradoxes of American literature: its naivety, its vigor, as well as the undeniable fact that it is now sometimes over-rated simply because it is American, and the culture of great power always has more sway (for itself, for others) than that of a minor country's, especially if its language becomes quasi-universal. But perhaps European experiments against realistic fiction, in the early part of the century (Gide, Pirandello, Surrealism and so on) were themselves part of an exhausted tradition. Sukenick has pleaded for an even more radical breakaway of American literature from its European roots, since America, with its many and enriching non-European elements, is culturally far wider than Europe, and certainly *all* dead and dying models are grist to its parody-mill: westerns are no longer made, the Gothic is over a century old, the gangster film long overtaken by life, SF weighed down by clichés and only here and there renewed, the realistic novel, by now a popular form, long declared dead, and only its most tired and nineteenth-century features parodied or stylized, etc. The lateness, then, is itself a naivety (hence the frequent fusions of stylization and model), which should regalvanize procedures, more vigorously, perhaps, than their more sophisticated European antecedents. Just as *Don Quixote*, a mock-romance long after the romance had died, was the beginning of modern fiction, or *Tristram Shandy,* the end and the beginning of the modern novel in one, so the result now should be a new strength, new forms, *even* realistic ones, stripped of their tired formulas and interpretive mania, merely showing the real, in its unique "idiocy," as the fantastic which it is. For ultimately *all* fiction is realistic, whether it mimes a mythic idea of heroic deeds or a progressive idea of society, or inner psychology, or, as now, the non-interpretability of the world, which is our reality as its interpretability once was (and may return). A fantastic realism. A new classicism, perhaps: *"nous vivons peut-être un pré-classicisme,"* as Gaëtan Picon said of Robbe-Grillet.

But not, I think, the romantic "New Gnosticism" Hassan rhapsodizes, whereby, according to McLuhan, Buckminster Fuller and others including, of course, Teilhard de Chardin who sparked it all off, the old gnostic dream and the new technological dream, after the present period of transition or disjunction, would converge toward a universal consciousness, the consciousness of God in Susan Sontag's terms, or the noonsphere in Chardin's (or perhaps, though I doubt that this is her meaning, beyond the "limits of the signifiable" in Kristeva's), the planet being as it were wrapped in telepathic or electronic thought of more and more brains working away. Hassan admits that the radical insufficiency of the human condition still offers intractable resistance to the old gnostic dream, and this resistance, he says, whether we call it evil (ananke) or The System, must be acknowledged without assent.

At the risk of siding with ananke or The System, I am less optimistic about the gnostic dream. This consciousness that is to wrap the planet seems to be dangerously like the pollution that may stifle it. For every work of incomparable genius in all fields there are millions of tons of paper wasted in garbage, in exactly the same way as every benefit of civilization is paid for not only in entropy but in pollution and extremely ugly politics to get hold of raw materials—what's left of them, not to mention the thousands of children's brains atrophied from lack of protein. The gnostic dream of the best scientific, technological and artistic brainstuff enveloping the earth seems to me essentially an elitist dream, akin to J. D. Bernal's (ironic, SF) suggestion that mankind may eventually divide into two species, the scientists and the others, the scientists colonizing the heaven but reverencing the earth as a sort of zoo (*The World, the Flesh and the Devil*, 1929), or else not far removed from Wells's collective mind or world-wide information service (*World Brain*, 1938), which presupposes an unprecedented harmony of minds: a mad and perhaps naive fusion of oblivion and utopia one could call oblitopia. Let the artists dream their gnostic or other dreams and produce verbal or other structures of them, but why, if art is to be regarded, in Hassan's words, as "no more nor less than anything else in life," should these dreams at the same time be given the supreme power of enveloping the planet (conquering the world), when neither those dreams nor man have shown the slightest capacity for solving the world's real problems, only a brilliant capacity for displacing them? At any rate, that envelope of brainstuff, more and more words and formulas and forms, continuous or discontinuous, theoretical or intuitive, not only seems to me yet another displacement, but also has me dead scared, even if like everyone else and in my infinitesimal way I am contributing to it, or to the garbage. I prefer to struggle more humbly inside that paradox, which to me is nevertheless the fundamental one today and the true symptom of mutation: the paradox of the liar who says he is a liar, the paradox of using words to say meaninglessness, the paradox of letting everyone *prendre la parole* when everyone knows that real power, whether political, economic, social, psychological or even mystical, functions silently and has no need of the semblance of speech, even though it never ceases to use that semblance to persuade us that we participate. If art can cope with that kind of terror and humor, it has a long future yet.

NOTES

1. The pagination refers to the English edition (London, Secker & Warburg, 1969).

2. In an opening address to a forum on Postmodernism at the Modern Language Association Conference, New York, 1978. The paper was read in a translated version, but for various reasons I have preferred to summarize and translate directly from the French original.

3. *Idiolect* is here used metaphorically, since often the modern criticism of poetry borrows linguistic terms (e.g., J. P. Thorne, 1963, on the poetry of Cummings, each poem producing its own "grammar" and being its own "idiolect"). Strictly speaking, *idiolect* is a language only its speaker understands (a contradiction in terms since language by definition communicates), for instance, a language one person has invented, for himself alone.

4. David Lodge, *The Modes of Modern Writing* (Ithaca, New York: Cornell University Press, 1977), p. 245.

5. Roland Barthes, *S/Z*, trans. Richard Howard (New York: Hill and Wang, 1974), pp. 44–45, 98, 139–40, 206.

What Are Experimental Novels and Why Are There So Many Left Unread?

Raymond Federman
SUNY, Buffalo

I am playing, of course—playing, on the title of Gertrude Stein's essay: "What Are Master-pieces and Why Are There So Few of Them?"

Once upon a time (not so long ago), when the novel was still respectable and respected, when there was even a place in the publishing marketplace for the so-called "experimental" novel (or what some people nowadays prefer to call "innovative" fiction), one was ashamed to admit not having read the latest novels.

It was indeed shameful to answer, No I have not, when asked, Have you read *Marjorie Morningstar?*—or let's say, since we are talking about serious fiction, Have you read *Lie Down in Darkness?* Yes, it was shameful to say, I have not!

Somehow, in those days, one felt guilty for not having read books—all the books, the good books (experimental or not). But then, why should a book make the reader feel guilty? Hell with it!

Then came a time when one would reply, unabashedly, No I have not read it yet, but I have read the reviews! This was the time when, in order to be, literature had to be ratified by the proper authorities.

Today, shamelessly, defiantly even, one answers when asked, Have you read John Barth's *Letters?* Oh I read about 40 pages of it . . . I could only go about ⅓ . . . I managed some 100 pages and then gave up . . . (There are of course exceptions—fanatics. Masochistic readers, or those whom Gore Vidal calls [*N.Y.R.B.*, 12/20/79]: ". . . gallant readers who risked their all in dubious battle with serious-texts, and failed—their names known only to whatever god makes the syllabus," and who have, Gore Vidal goes on, "the courage to read a book that could not, very simply, be read at all by anyone, ever.")

And the same usually goes for novels like *Ada* (Nabokov), *Gravity's Rainbow* (Pynchon), *JR* (Gaddis), *Mulligan Stew* (Sorrentino), but these are BIG books (though I fail to see how the size/length/weight of a book affect its readability!). But what about the novels/stories of Walter Abish, Steve Katz, Ronald Sukenick, Clarence Major, George Chambers, and many others who do not write BIG books, and yet are declared unreadable?

The question then: Is a novel labeled "unreadable" because it is experimental (*a priori* or *a posteriori*)? Or is it labeled "experimental" because it is left unread?

E X P E R I M E N T A L—it says: therefore an easy excuse to walk away from the book—to walk out on a novel, and thus fail to assume the consequences of one's relations with the text. How irresponsible: to render invalid the writer/text/reader contract (especially if you have paid your $9.95, $12.95, $16.95 for the damn thing).

Perhaps the time has come again to ask, What is an experiment? Perhaps it is time to go back to the source and check the exact definition, and thus avoid any further confusion.

In my (Unabridged) *Webster's Third New International Dictionary*, p. 800:

> Experiment: *n.* 1 a: a test or trial (make another ∼ of his suspicion—Shak.)
>
> b (1): a tentative procedure or policy; *esp*: one adopted in uncertainty as to whether it will answer the desired purpose or bring about the desired result (he is going to put his hope to the test by trying an ∼ of bold proportions—Harold Callender) (2): the tangible result of such a procedure or policy (Benavente's earliest literary ∼s were four little romantic fantasies . . . published in 1892—*Current Biog*) c: an act or operation carried out under conditions determined by the experimenter (as in a laboratory) in order to discover some unknown principle or effect or to test, establish, or illustrate some suggested or known truth (the ∼s of the defendant's experts lead . . . to the opinion that a typhoid bacillus could not survive the journey—O. W. Holmes, †1935) 2 *obs*: experience (by sad ∼ I know how little weight my words with thee can find—John Milton) 3 *obs*: expedient, remedy (you will find it a sure ∼ for the quinsy—William Coles) 4 : the process or practice of trying or testing: experimentation (the result of some centuries of ∼ tended to raise rather than silence doubt—Henry Adams)

How interesting! How fascinating! Amazing how these definitions always speak to the point (and not without some appropriate irony) and speak for themselves.

I reflect, my thoughts spinning, skipping, HOPSCOTCHing (as always playgiaristically):

The usual novel misses its mark because it limits the reader to its own ambit; the better defined it is, the better the novelist is thought to be. We should attempt on the other hand a text that would not clutch the reader but which would oblige him to become an accomplice as it whispers to him underneath the conventional exposition other more esoteric directions. A narrative that will not be a pretext for the transmission of a message—(there is no message, only messengers, and that is the message, just as love is the one who loves).

Lunch with some colleagues from the English Department (one cannot spend all day thinking, writing, messing around with dictionaries). We are talking shop:

"What are you teaching this semester?" I ask V. D. to make conversation.

"A graduate seminar on the Contemporary American Novel," V. D. answers.

I am interested. I go on: "What are you reading?"

"Oh some Bellow, Malamud, Singer, Roth, Heller, Gardner, and the new Styron. You know, the usual."

"If it were not for the last two," I say, not being facetious at all, "it could be a course on the Jewish Novel . . . No Barth?"

"Yes, in fact, an early one. *The End of the Road.*"

"What about Pynchon? *Gravity's Rainbow*! It's an important book, I think."

I like V. D., he's a serious scholar, and a good buddy (we play tennis together once a week). ". . . and what about Hawkes, Gass, Coover," I hesitate, "Sukenick?"

"Oh that stuff is unreadable!" V. D. says with a grimace on his face.

Unreadable! (He must be annoyed with me, I beat him 6-2, 6-1, last week.) How does an English professor determine what is readable and what is unreadable? I do not say that, I merely think that, to myself. "And what about you? What are you teaching?" I ask C. B.

"An undergraduate course on the Modern European Novel."

I am fascinated. I visualize the poor sophomores struggling with Philippe Sollers, Maurice Roche, Georges Pérec, Ludovic Janvier . . . (The beast in me thinks French these days and besides I often regress into the safety of my native tongue whenever speaking of contemporary fiction).

"We're going to start with Joyce's *The Portrait*," C. B. volunteers while chewing at his Tiffinburger, "then Kafka's *Metamorphosis*, one Camus, I'm not sure which one yet, then one or two other Germans (C. B. has a Ph.D. in Comparative Literature, Anglo/German), Günter Grass, maybe Heinrich Böll, and then we'll finish with one Beckett, an early one, *Murphy*, I suppose, the later novels are too obscure. You know, six or seven novels."

"Not a bad reading list . . . No Calvino though? You know, *Cosmicomics, T/Zero, Invisible Cities.*" I throw these in to impress my colleagues.

"That stuff is too difficult, too tedious for undergraduates." C. B. has finished his hamburger deluxe and is now sipping his coffee. "I'm not sure they would get anything out of reading these books. And besides they don't have the necessary background."

Ah yes, the question of necessity!

Gertrude Stein again: "Therefore a master-piece [here you may substitute, if you wish, experimental novel for the occasion without assuming, however, that all experimental novels are master-pieces, far from it] has essentially not be necessary, it has to be that is it has to exist but it does not have to be necessary it is not in response to necessity as action is because the minute it is necessary it has in it no possibility of going on."

Exactly! Why bother then with Unreadability? Especially when it isn't necessary, and there is so much "Readable stuff" around.

But what is Readability? I can't resist—here we go again, back to my *Webster's*: "Readable: . . . that can be read with ease . . . legible . . . pleasing, interesting, or offering no great difficulty to the reader . . . clear in details and significance of symbols . . . that can be read throughout."

I see! Readability then: what is clear, easy, legible, pleasing, interesting, in other words, what reassures us in a text (a novel) of what we already know, what comforts us because we easily and pleasurably recognize the world (at a glance) and ourselves in the world (at another glance) in what we read. Readability: what is instantly and clearly recognizable, and thus orients us within ourselves and outside of ourselves within the "reality" of the world. Readability: what guides us back from the text to the world, to the security of the world, and therefore gives us comfort—the pleasure of easy recognition!

Of course: "The author cannot chose to write *what will not be read.*

And yet, it is the very rhythm of what is read and what is not read that creates the pleasure of the great narratives: has anyone ever read Proust, Balzac, *War and Peace*, word for word? (Proust's good fortune: from one reading to the next, we never skip the same passages)." That, I suppose, is what is meant by *The Pleasure of the Text*: ". . . what I enjoy in a narrative is not directly its content or even its structure, but rather the abrasions I impose upon the fine surface: I read on, I skip, I look up, I dip in again."

But there is a paradox here (and Roland Barthes knows this): "Read slowly, read *all* of a novel by Zola, and the book will drop from your hands; read fast, in snatches, some modern text [let's say John Barth's *Letters*], and it becomes opaque, inaccessible to your pleasure: you want something to happen and nothing does, for *what happens to the language does not happen to the discourse*."

First conclusion: If "Readability" is *the pleasure of recognition* (easy pleasurable referential recognition), then "Unreadability" is *the agony of unrecognition*.

Unreadability: what disorients us in a text (especially in an experimental novel) in relation to ourselves (and I do not mean here the bulk, the degree of difficulty, the self-reflexiveness, the tediousness of the text—these are weak excuses). Unreadability: what prevents us from recognizing that something is happening, but also prevents us from looking up and away from the text, what locks us into the language.

Imagine then how lost, how confused, how desperate a reader must feel when reading a text where "nothing happens twice," as in some Beckett novels or plays, or where the language moves in a nonsensical direction and therefore means-not, as in some Barthelme stories, or where everything "changes like a cloud as it goes," as in a Sukenick novel, or where everything cancels out, as in my own *Take It or Leave It* (excuse the narcissistic reference, but the beast in me often thinks intertextually when writing about experimental fiction).

But then "writing is not the living repetition of life," I insist, and one should add, "reading is always done haphazardly."

The pleasure that a text affords us then is that of recognizing our own knowledge in it, our own culture rather (I'm paraphrasing here)—of recognizing (righteously) how cultivated we are, and consequently how total, how coherent, continuous, rational, how whole, how secure we are in our culture. The readable novel reassures us of that.

But what about the Unreadable novel? And precisely, Roland Barthes in *The Pleasure of the Text* makes a crucial distinction between these two types of texts:

1) "Text of pleasure: the text that contents, fills, grants euphoria; the text that comes from culture and does not break with it, is linked to a *comfortable* practice of reading." That then would be the readable novel.

2) "Text of bliss: the text that imposes a state of loss, the text that discomforts (perhaps to the point of a certain boredom), unsettles the reader's historical, cultural, psychological assumptions, the consistency of his tastes, values, memories, brings to a crisis his relations with language." The unreadable novel—better known in the supermarket of books as "the experimental novel."

And so here we have it! Second conclusion: a) The usual (readable) novel, that which "is linked to a comfortable practice of reading" and preserves culture. b) The experimental (unreadable) novel, that which "brings to a crisis the reader's relations with language" and undermines culture.

But there is more to this: That comfortableness of readability is there because the text sends the reader back to reality, or allows the reader to play his little mental cinema of realism beyond the language. And so, once again, readability is equated with reality—and lately, even with "Morality."

Deny reality, cut off the referential paths to reality, and your novel will become unreadable, and to be unreadable, these days, is immoral!

Reflect on your language, write language, examine your relations with language within the mirrors of the text, and you are immediately denounced, accused, and found guilty of "experimentation," and therefore declared unreadable!

The true writer, we are told, writes about people, real people, things and events, he does not write on writing, he uses words, but does not reflect on them, does not make of words the object of his ruminations. The true writer will be anything but an anatomist of language. The dissection of language is the fancy of those who, having nothing to write, write about writing, and thus create useless and immoral "word-structures." And the watchdogs of culture and morality are quick to point out that such activities "may be dismissed as little more than the obligatory hyperbole of avant-garde self-promotion, the upping of the ante of extremism that seems necessary now in order to be heard above the competitive din."

Of course those who say that are usually those (the 40-pagers) who have never really read an experimental novel in its entirety, and that merely for the protection of their own moral good health. But nonetheless they are quick to advise the novelist to write what you see, what you know, what you remember, if you want to be read(able), for if you write what you do not see, what you do not know, what you do not remember, you will certainly be unread(able).

Yet, contradictably, those who deplore that *Literature* has turned *Against Itself* because it is only concerned with its language, the "corruption of language," and not with social, political and historical reality (or what is still known as Humanism), are willing to concede (since they have no other choice in serious fiction today, and I suppose to save face within the great fiasco of reality) that perhaps novelists should at least attempt to describe the "unreality of reality," if that's where we are now. Anything to preserve the mimetic imposture. But that's like asking an abstract painter (a Clyfford Still, for instance) to paint little recognizable objects and subjects in his paintings so that one can at least *see* something besides paint.

Now some people might say that this situation is not very encouraging, but one must reply that it is not meant to encourage those who say that—usually out of despair.

Or as Gertrude Stein explains: "All this sounds awfully complicated, but it is not complicated at all, it is just what happens. Any of you when you write you try to remember what you are about to write and you will see immediately how lifeless the writing becomes that is why expository writing is so dull because it is all remembered, that is why illustration is so dull because you remember what somebody looked like and you make your illustration look like it. The minute your memory functions while you are doing anything it may be very popular but actually it is dull. And that is what a master-piece is not (here again make same substitution as before), it may be unwelcome but it is never dull."

This brings us to reflect further on the novel in our time: Can it be said that by denouncing the fraudulence of a "usual" novel which tends to totalize existence and misses its pluridimensionality the experimental work in a way frees us from the illusion of realism?

I rather believe that it encloses us in it. Because the goal remains the same: it is always a question of expressing, of translating something which is already there—even if to be already there, in this new perspective, consists paradoxically in not being there.

In other words, the novel, in a sense, cannot escape realism, for language too is *a* reality. This mortgage weighs upon it since its origin (and not only since the nineteenth century), since the period when, in order to justify itself from the suspicion of frivolity, it had to present itself as a means of knowledge.

However, let's not kid ourselves, reality as such has never really interested anyone; it is and has always been a form of disenchantment. What makes reality fascinating at times is the imaginary catastrophe which hides behind it. The writer knows this and exploits it.

Do you believe for a moment that power, economy, war, peace, sex, all the great tricks of reality (and many others too) would have held for a single moment without the fascination which sustains them, and which comes to them, in fact, from the inverted mirror in which they are reflected—a fascination that comes from the endless reversion, the sensitive and imminent bliss of their catastrophe? Especially today when reality is but a stockpile of dead matter, dead bodies, dead language.

Edgar Allan Poe was so right in his time when he called nascent nineteenth-century realism that pitiable stuff invented by merchants for the depiction of decayed cheeses.

The history of the novel is nothing else but the success of its efforts to "appresent" and not "represent" a reality which always evades, always substitutes for vulgar mirrors, finer mirrors—more selective mirrors.

But in another sense, the novel is nothing else but a denunciation, by its very reality, of the illusion which animates it. All great novels are critical novels (that is to say, experimental novels) which, under the pretense of telling a story, of bringing characters to life, of interpreting situations, slide under our eyes the mirage of a tangible form. From its "unthinkable" beginning to its "impossible" end, all fictitious *work* forms a block, an autonomous block; nothing can be taken away from it nor can anything be changed in it. That is what makes of the novel a lure.

We think we are going to find in it the expression of our unity, whereas in fact it only manifests the desire of it. We believe, as we are relating ourselves (and being related), that we are going to discover, to find, that being that we are already. But that being, that somebody, exists inside the work only, and not outside: it is the product of it, and not the source. And this because the essence of a literary discourse (experimental or not is finally irrelevant)—that is to say a discourse fixed once and for all (whether we like it or not, read it or not)—is to find its own point of reference, its own rules of organization in itself, and not in the real or imaginary experience on which it rests.

Through all the detours that one wishes, the subject who writes will never seize himself in the novel: he will only seize the novel which, by definition, excludes him. And that, of course, is also true of the reader.

And so—final conclusion—as Gertrude Stein writes: "Always it is true that the master-piece [experimental novel again] has nothing to do with *human nature* or with *identity*, it has to do with the *human mind* and the *entity* that is with a thing in itself and not in relation" (my italics).

And that is WHY THERE ARE SO MANY EXPERIMENTAL NOVELS LEFT UNREAD!

Relativism and the Multiple Contexts for Contemporary Fiction

Geoffrey Green
University of Southern California

To begin, let us consider a plot: a recently-married woman decides that her husband is intolerable and must be eliminated; resolving to murder him, the wife confides in her best friend. The two women plot to kill the fellow and share the insurance premium. After fastidious preparation and analysis, they make the following attempts, all of which fail: they mix LSD in the batter of his French toast, hoping that the husband will hallucinate while driving and initiate a fatal car accident; the venomous sac of a tarantula is slipped into a slice of black-berry pie, but the young man inadvertently pushes the poison off to the side of the plate without consuming it; a naked electric cord is thrown into the man's shower while he is washing, but the result proves inef-fective; while the husband sleeps, they try to shoot an air bubble into his vein with a hypodermic syringe in order to induce heart failure, but the tip of the syringe breaks; they place bullets in the carburetor of his truck; they search for poisonous snakes without any luck. . . .

But it is not necessary to continue with this. The consistent nature of the murder attempts is sufficiently apparent. Are we dealing with a modern attempt to evoke the Borgias? Or a particularly indulgent parlor room detective story? No, we are retelling the actual testimony from a murder trial several years ago in San Diego. And I think it can be seen that these two young women were suffering from a failure of the imagination. The decision to wrench their lives out of the compla-cent banalities they no doubt embodied could inspire from them only a rehashing of tired and grotesque, impractical and therefore comic, lit-erary plots drawn from popular novels, television melodramas, films, radio, and comic books. Although obviously familiar with the endings of these earlier fiascos, they stubbornly cling to the belief that in their

33

hands, the tools will succeed; the immediate and subjectively awesome perception that the husband must be killed transcended their objective awareness that their schemes were impractical, dream-like.

When they persistently met with failure, they did not realize, with abruptness, that their viewpoint was awry; the ultimate dream of the insurance money in a world-without-the-husband was invested with such romantic allure that they simply switched plots: they heroically jumped from Dorothy Sayers into the proceedings of a tough-guy Raymond Chandler novel. They bludgeoned the man to death with a six and one-half pound lead weight, then tossed him off a bridge. Even in this realm, their sense of borrowed bathos, of loyalty to previous forms did not desert them; the wife's friend recalled that she said out loud "I'm sorry, Dave," as she repeatedly struck the young man. Even the ending was predictable: horrified by the bleeding, they taped the man's ears and forgot to remove it.

All of us are doubtless more aware than the two women that we are participants in the movement of history. Any pretenses toward the making of objectively true judgements about a process we are *in* remains an illusion and a cherished dream. Our modern sensibility insists upon extreme relativism; and yet how many of us are able to resist the temptation to bestow absolute evaluations upon the specialized studies we care the most about? All too frequently, we cling to our hard-won subjectivity—and then advocate it as being objective. So, for instance, many were shocked and horrified by Robert Gorham Davis's attack on the New Critics in 1951 when he suggested that their critical stance was not purely organic but represented an attempt to negate the stature of democratic and popular authors of the past and to discourage such writers in the present.[1] But an awareness of historical relativism and currents of intellectual dialectics would predict such a response, and anticipate it.

Once we have weathered an era we are always amazed by the salient aspects which become apparent only as the period ends. But those "insights" are tied not only to the period about which they are concerned, but also to the period which engenders them. In 1923, Leon Trotsky wrote to denigrate the Russian Formalist school of criticism:

> The Formalists do not carry their idea of art to its logical conclusion. If one is to regard the process of poetic creation only as a combination of sounds or words . . . then the only perfect formula of "poetics" will be this: Arm yourself with a dictionary and create by means of algebraic combinations and

permutations of words, all the poetic works of the world which have not yet been created.[2]

Trotsky's understanding of the principles which bolster the Formalist school was crude and minimal; indeed, it can be maintained that he was not even aware of the implications of the Formalist methodology—he was concerned only with the absence of an activist Marxist commitment in the Formalist writings. He meant his statement, therefore, to be both reductive and provocative; unfair, and yet annoyingly apt. He would have had only a negative interest in Hugh Kenner's influential essay, "Art in a Closed Field," which appeared in 1962:

> For centuries literature, like arithmetic, was supposed to be, in a direct and naive way, "about" the familiar world. . . . But lately we have been getting what amounts to the shifting of elements and postulates inside a closed field.[3]

Kenner noted further that when we "drop the assumption that novels are more about people than they are about things" and relate, instead, to this mathematical analogy of a "closed field," we will gain insights into modern literary art and make key "discoveries" about it.

Kenner's articulate essay contributed greatly to the preliminary understanding of a flux of novels which began to appear in the Sixties; his article, like other attempts to conceive of this fiction which seemed to assault traditional and accepted notions about literary form and genre, was of a piece with the time and decade of its inception.

By now it should not be surprising to note that one answer to Kenner appeared in 1967 with Carl Oglesby's "The Deserters: The Contemporary Defeat of Fiction." Oglesby suggested that "literature is most essentially a form of history, something which makes propositions about the human experience . . . which ought to be . . . significant and . . . true." Oglesby sought to denigrate literature which was excessively "elegant," concerned with itself as form rather than as idea; he charged that the rebellion broached in the existentialism of Camus was only a gauze concealing a reactionary political stance. Novels such as Joseph Heller's *Catch 22* create "a world in which the summons to partisanship has been muffled if not ridiculed by a nihilism which has recently discovered gaiety, a despair which has learned how to frolic in the ruins of a certain hope."[4]

Oglesby concludes with an attack upon "post-realistic" fiction, but

how many of us recall that term? or its various siblings and antecedents? Whatever the term, the argument assumes the dimensions of a
debate about the prevailing nature of art: something beautiful, meant
to be contemplated, and therefore, useless and frivolous; or else, something cognitive and functional, activist, and therefore, meaningful and
conscience-bound. Oglesby claims that it is a lie to assert:

> that after reality there might still be something left. There will not be.
> There will only be men who can catch an eternally difficult reality and those
> who cannot. Those who cannot will continue to conceal their desertion be-
> neath an historical sadness endlessly more intricate in design and in decora-
> tion even lovely: we shall continue to hear the sighs of an expiring culture
> whose self-confidence is being permanently broken.[5]

Is the novel historical and purposeful or organic and self-contained?
The entire discussion was relative to the intellectual climate and prevailing trends of thought of our previous decades. And yet the debate
has existed in other periods and within other contexts. Oglesby need not
have worried: many readers were able to enjoy Heller's novel and simultaneously develop an activism which included political protest and
demonstrations. The immediate examples and transient manifestations
of the argument have faded from our central attention; what remains is
the argument itself. And perhaps it is not even an argument, for there
is really no choice.

The human need to characterize and mythologize is behind our attempt to label in exemplary fashion the prevailing trends of prior decades, or prior literary movements. The roaring Twenties, the depres-
sion Thirties, the World War II Forties are clearly compartmentalized
within our minds, but were the Fifties "happy days," or repressive and
asleep? Were the Sixties political and activist, or mystical and religious, as Tom Wolfe recently claimed?[6] It is impressive that as we approach our own historical situation our efforts fail (like the two mur-
derous young women from San Diego, our contemporaries). Not one
trendy magazine writer has succeeded in providing a catchy or pervasive label or meaning for our present decade or the Seventies which pre-
ceded it. All of this should tell us something, and perhaps the time is
appropriate to gently reappraise what we consider our literature to be,
at a time when more people are writing fiction than ever before in our
history, and fewer people are reading it. At least we are now able to understand Robert Musil's words about his great novel *The Man Without*

Qualities: "Events, anyhow, are interchangeable. I am interested in what is typical, and in what one might call the ghostly aspect of reality."[7]

Instead of focusing exclusively upon mimetic vs. anti-mimetic, traditional vs. innovative, beautiful vs. functional modes of understanding, let us turn to the problem posed by Jorge Luis Borges's story, "The Secret Miracle."[8] Ostensibly, the fiction provides an account of the arrest and execution by the Nazis of an Eastern European writer. We are told that he was shot on March 29, 1943, at 9:02 a.m. We are also told that he was being killed because the Nazis, knowing nothing of his literary pursuits, mistakenly believed him to be significant and threatening; they take seriously the preposterously over-bloated claims of a catalog which had been written to sell many editions of his books. Although we share much of the prisoner's anguish before death, the fiction leads us to a consideration of his literary works, one of which was in-progress. This play, "The Enemies," cancels itself out; in effect, it never occurs as action, but rather as "the circular delirium" within a deranged mind which has assumed the identity and existence of another man. Borges tells us that this play, for the writer, "held the possibility of allowing him to redeem (symbolically) the meaning of his life" (p. 91). He prays to God for an additional year of life in order to complete his play. On the morning of his execution, he is marched out and positioned against a wall; the soldiers raise their rifles; a drop of rain falls on his cheek; the order to fire is given.

At this moment, Borges reveals that "the physical universe came to a halt" (p. 93). Nothing moves: the rifles remain poised, the drop clings to the man's cheek; but he realizes that "God had worked a secret miracle for him, German lead would kill him at the set hour, but in his mind a year would go by between the order and its execution" (p. 93). In gratitude, and with a detached leisure, the author works and reworks his conception until, precisely at the end of his subjectively-perceived year, he completes his play. And in the same moment, the rain drop resumes its descent, the rifles fire, and the author falls dead.

What interests me in this story is the final scene and the vision which underscores it. In that instant that is an entire year, in that frozen and motionless chronology, we focus upon a writer who "was not working for posterity or even for God, whose literary tastes were unknown to him. Meticulously, motionlessly, secretly, he wrought in time his lofty, invisible labyrinth" (p. 94). And it appears to me that

Borges's conceit provides us with a device for conceiving of the realms
implicit in the creation of a literary work. On the one hand, we have,
in the order for execution, an example of the fateful and awesome procession of chronology, the ominous and inescapable dictum of historical determinism.

On the other hand, we discern in the author's unfinished play the su-
premely subjective and individualistic realm all of us nurture against
the intrusion of oppressive external reality—our internal flow of
thoughts, private creations, and dreams. Now it seems to me that
Oglesby and company would argue that the moment of one's death is
apocalyptic and absolute. The concern for an unfinished piece of literary fluff would appear to be some perverse and decadent
joke—especially in the face of such an odious and malignant instrument of human oppression. If the author had not wasted his time with
his play and had joined in the struggle for political freedom, he might
never have been against the wall awaiting his death and wishing for another year; instead, he would have the natural duration of his life to indulge in literary composition, once the common enemy was destroyed
and all men were blessed with basic liberties, etc. Similarly, it is not
difficult for me to conceive of a scholar trained to view literature as a
hermetic enterprise one day discovering a play such as "The Enemies":
in a brief, but devastating, introductory paragraph to his critical essay
he would attack the odious meanness which resulted in the wasteful
loss of the author's life; then, he would devote the rest of the piece to a
brilliant analysis of the play-at-hand.

But neither of these positions accurately describes the scene in
Borges's story. Between the realms of collective society and the individual imagination lurks the author, crucially attached to both sources,
but curiously transcending them both. The author-in-time and his creative result (which is both *in* time and eternal; both material and ideal)
mediate between the competing necessities and demands of our lives
and our dreams. And although all of the realms intersect and wreak
their effects upon the other, the act of literary creation, the construction of verbal edifices, is corporeally dependent upon society and the
imagination, and simultaneously, eternal and independent. So we find
Borges's author—or any author—"motionless," yet "in time," creating
that work of literary art which will confirm his existence and justify
him: even as he confronts the end of his life.

Further, it is the precise conjuncture of all three realms which best exemplifies our present sense of the process of literary creation. Our understanding of and investigation into the nature of works of literature would, necessarily, involve a comprehensive and multi-disciplined effort to situate the author and his words in relation to the author's (and our own) exigent reality and dreams; we would seek to discern the relative emphasis as it was meted out to each affiliative realm. Accordingly, this focus can provide for certain alterations in our sense of literary evolution. Genres, for instance, can be viewed as collective societal constraints upon the individual impulses of each writer. One example which comes to mind is Wolfgang Hildesheimer's story, "A World Ends," which was acclaimed in Europe as a militant political attack upon those hypocritical and snobbish intellectuals who celebrate the "cult of the antique and forgotten," and was admired here as an elaborate spinning of an excessively ornate and deliberately fatuous web of prose, designed so that it would unravel at the moment of dramaturgical emphasis.[9] Actually, neither view does justice to the artistry, but the attention is justified: this narrative about an artificially-constructed island devoted to the celebration of spurious art and the passive reactions of its residents as the island sinks is an attempt to situate art between action and contemplation; it interpolates literary creation between the reality of form and the dream of formlessness.

The point is that an enormous, diverse, and enigmatic assortment of novels and works of fiction all seem to coalesce about the realm of intersection which includes the author, his creation, his imagination, and the surrounding world. And the contributing authors are aware of this emphasis and attempt to focus upon it.

A suitable example is John Hawkes's brilliant novel, *The Lime Twig*. A good deal of critical attention has been focused upon this novel as a fictional projection of a highly individualistic imaginative vision. Although written in the third person voice, it begins with the monologue of a powerful and engrossing first person narrator; this character, Hencher, is gratuitously killed off in the opening third of the novel. The innocent heroine, Margaret Banks, is captured, raped, and brutally beaten with a heavy rubber truncheon for no apparent reason. Explanations for these occurrences have followed Hawkes's lead (enunciated in countless interviews), dwelling upon the importance of mythic symbolism in his work, emphasizing surreal nightmare imagery, the mining of the creative unconscious, the obsessiveness of the authorial sensibility.

Without minimizing the importance of these themes of artistic creativity for Hawkes and his readers, it is yet necessary to underscore the way in which *The Lime Twig* functions as a depiction of an author actively wrestling with the inherent conventions of his genre. In *The Lime Twig*, Hawkes envisioned his purpose: "to parody the soporific plot of the thriller." Hencher's death, however, was "an appropriate violation of fictional expectation or fictional 'rules.' "[10] Thus, Hencher's death—strange, peculiar, whimsical—has been celebrated as a creative flouting of novelistic conventions. But apart from this aspect, Hencher's death—and the switch in point of view from Hencher to Michael and Margaret Banks—has a structural coherence if we look back to the thriller which Hawkes parodies by weaving the names of its characters into his text: Graham Greene's *Brighton Rock*.[11]

There are many shared details which suggest that Hawkes was looking back at the Greene novel. Besides the obvious similarity as to horse racing and gangsters, Hawkes incorporates Greene's fictional characters into his novel: Pinkie, the young mobster, becomes "Pinky Lane," a street; Ida Arnold, known as Lily, occurs as "Lily Eastchip," Hencher's landlady; Pinkie's wife, Rose, is, in *The Lime Twig*, "Reggie's Rose," the nude woman painted on the side of the crashed airplane which Hencher explores. Similarly, to mirror the newspaperman Kolly Kibber of *Brighton Rock*, there is Sidney Slyter whose column helps organize the novel.

Greene's *Brighton Rock* begins from the point of view of Charles Hale, a newspaperman who is running for his life from the mob; when he is murdered in the opening section of the book, the narrative switches to the point of view of: Pinkie, the thug who killed Hale; Rose, the girl who loves Pinkie; and Ida, the woman who pursues Hale's murderer. Thus, *The Lime Twig* is fashioned so as to reflect, incorporate, and parody the generic ingredients of *Brighton Rock*: Hencher's obsessive recollections mirror Hale's tormented thoughts; Hencher's premature death (in terms of the structure of the novel) is tailored to the killing of Hale at the end of the first section of Greene's novel; Hale is murdered for interfering in the rackets of the Brighton gangs; Hencher is killed partially in punishment for his deliberate neglect of his mother after she experienced severe burns during a suspicious fire. The deaths of both characters signal an integral shift in the narrative perspective of each work.

Brighton Rock is not the only thriller parodied by *The Lime Twig*. Eric

Ambler's *Background to Danger* helps provide a generic context for the brutal beating of Margaret Banks by the gangster, Thick. Thick uses a truncheon, a weapon popular in the Thirties setting of Ambler's novel, but practically nonexistent in the Fifties and early Sixties of Hawkes's England. Here is a passage from Ambler, as the protagonist Kenton is being tortured by the sadistic Captain Mailler:

> The Captain . . . had taken the rubber truncheon from his pocket and was weighing it in his hand and flicking it viciously against the side of the arch. It made almost no sound. Kenton looked at Mailler's face. An unpleasant change had come over it. The jaw had dropped slightly, his cheeks were sunken, he was breathing rather quickly and kept darting little sidelong glances at Kenton with eyes that had become curiously glazed. . . .
>
> Suddenly, he lifted the truncheon high into the air and went up on his toes. Kenton clenched his teeth. The truncheon came down with lightning speed and stopped an inch from his cheek.
>
> . . . [Mailler] tapped the side of Kenton's head playfully with the truncheon. It was cold and had a certain hard greasiness about it.[12]

Now here is a portion of the description of Margaret's beating by Thick—made more sparse and poetic, but treading the same generic path:

> He reached down for her and she felt the truncheon nudging against her thigh, gently, like a man's cane in a crowd. . . .
>
> Then something happened to his face. To the mouth really. The sour sweat was there and the mouth went white, so rigid and distended that for a moment he couldn't speak. . . .
>
> His arm went up quivering, over his head with the truncheon falling back, and came down hard and solid as a length of cold fat stripped from a pig. . . . It made a sound like a dead bird falling to empty field.[13]

Finally, Margaret's ordeal—narrated after the fact from her own point of view—is anticipated by the after-the-fact narration from Kenton's point of view of his earlier beating. (Ambler: "Now, nearly twelve hours of sleep had left him wondering why on earth he had made such a lot of fuss. If they wanted the wretched photographs, let them have them. All that absurd fit of heroics had produced was a swollen lip and a bruised face. A nice mess he had landed himself in!"[14] Hawkes: "It was 4 a.m. in the darkness that had begun with bees and warbling and the fading of bells, and Thick had used the ropes. . . . She knew there was enormous penalty for what they had done to her—but she could not conceive of that, did not require that:

she only wanted a little comfort, a bit of charity; with the awfulness, the unknowable, removed."[15])

In Ambler's novel, the fascist Mailler inflicts his brutality upon the progressive Kenton, only to lose in the end: this was readily evident to contemporary readers. But Hawkes erases the ideological distinctions while maintaining a moral distinction: the good Margaret suffers at the hands of the evil thugs—and there is no poetic justice. Thus, the parody is subtle and provocative: it centers upon a beating which in both novels is obligatory, but for Hawkes, the generic necessity dictates the novel's dramatic proceedings and the world is depicted as being remote and predetermined.

The point is that John Hawkes's *The Lime Twig* is a work designed to be perceived as an imaginative artistic vision formulated by an author aware of previous authors and their artistic contributions within a fluid and evolving genre. The process of meaningfully parodying a form—in this case, the thriller—necessitates the utilization of specific earlier texts; these are used to create a new text which exploits the generic form by forging a new fictional vision upon what was earlier perceived as formal conventions and in so doing, transcends them. Our estimation of Hawkes is not diminished by this realization; indeed, our sense of his originality is heightened by the extent to which his creative vision was conceived as an amalgam of personal, literary, and social forces.

It is always tempting to insinuate that a perceived phenomenon is confirmative of a movement, or an artistic vortex, but everything which contributes to our perception of an exciting and essential "contemporary reformation" decries such an assertion. It is not altogether clear to me why so much admirable fiction is being written at the present time, but I would guess that it is inspired not only by an active contemporary revival in critical theory, but by the pervasive modern insight, relevant to both movements, that our lives are composed of relativistic contingencies, deprived of any ultimate coherence. And if that is the case, then our lives and the events which comprise them become—in Musil's word— "interchangeable"; certainly, that is a subjective realization sufficiently potent to inspire enthusiasm for the alternative of creating a differentiated fictional world.

I am relatively certain, however, that a familiarity with contemporary fiction and its deliberate territory of operation can lead to exciting moments of vision, as when a fiction which might on its own merit have been termed "innovative" appears among the works of an author who previously might have been termed "traditional." Little attention has been paid to Chekov's "The Black Monk,"[16] probably because it resists the label "social realistic" which so often has been applied to his work. But we can see in that fiction—about an author who shirks his worldly affairs in order to dwell in a realm characterized by a mystical black monk (first one, then geometrically-increasing numbers of black monks), an obsession which inspires a rampant creative prolificity and an accompanying contempt for all life-supporting functions: so that at the moment of his death he is infused with an artistic revelation of a grotesque world populated with demonic black monks, and yet simultaneously, a feeling of buoyant healthiness—an affiliation with Borges's "The Secret Miracle."

A process is here being described, and it does not simply extend forward, or owe its only ancestry to the literary past. Rather, we have here an authorial mode of vision which has always and naturally been present. And because this vision expresses itself in fiction yet emanates from all of our shared need for fictions to mediate between our inner and outer worlds, we are participants in this contemporary reformation: intensely so, it would seem, in our present day, when our yearning for sustenance and meaning is desperate and profound, and our faith in our subjective abilities has been discouraged and minimized.

Even from a posture of extreme relativism, we can believe certain things: that there is, for instance, in the words of William Carlos Williams, a "jump between fact and the imaginative reality,"[17] and that the forceful constructions of words may well be our mediation between them. Let us conclude by listening as Italo Calvino, certainly one of the most forceful of these contemporary authors, describes the felt nature of the process we have been examining:

> Literature is a combinational game which plays on the possibilities intrinsic to its own material, independently of the personality of the author. But it is also a game which at a certain stage is invested with an unexpected meaning, a meaning having no preference at the linguistic level on which the activity takes place, but which springs from another level and brings into play something on that other level that means a great deal to the author or to the society of which he is a member.[18]

NOTES

1. Robert Gorham Davis, "The New Criticism and the Democratic Tradition," *American Scholar*, 19 (Winter 1950–51).

2. Leon Trotsky, "The Formalist School of Poetry and Marxism," in *Marxists on Literature: An Anthology*, ed. David Craig (Baltimore: Penguin, 1975), pp. 370–71.

3. Hugh Kenner, "Art in a Closed Field," in *Learners and Discerners: A Newer Criticism*, ed. Robert Scholes (Charlottesville: University of Virginia Press, 1964), p. 124.

4. Carl Oglesby, "The Deserters: The Contemporary Defeat of Fiction," in *Radical Perspectives in the Arts*, ed. Lee Baxandall (Baltimore: Penguin, 1972), p. 35.

5. Ibid., p. 51.

6. Tom Wolfe, "The Spirit of the Age," in his *Mauve Gloves and Madmen, Clutter and Vine* (New York: Bantam, 1977), pp. 94–147.

7. Cited in Georg Lukács, *Realism in our Time: Literature and the Class Struggle* (New York: Harper and Row, 1971), p. 25.

8. Jorge Luis Borges, "The Secret Miracle," trans. Harriet de Onís, in his *Labyrinths: Selected Stories and Other Writings* (New York: New Directions, 1964), pp. 88–94. All subsequent textual references refer to this edition and are cited in the paper.

9. Wolfgang Hildesheimer, "A World Ends," trans. Christopher Holme in *Great German Short Stories*, ed. Stephen Spender (New York: Dell, 1960; 8th ed., 1971), pp. 278–84.

10. "Interview with John Hawkes," in *The Contemporary Writer: Interviews with Sixteen Novelists and Poets*, ed. L. S. Dembo and Cyrena N. Pondrom (Madison: The University of Wisconsin Press, 1972), p. 13.

11. Graham Greene, *Brighton Rock* (1938; New York: Bantam, 1968).

12. Eric Ambler, *Background to Danger* (1937; New York: Bantam, 1973), pp. 84–85.

13. John Hawkes, *The Lime Twig* (New York: New Directions, 1961), pp. 127–29.

14. Ambler, p. 77.

15. Hawkes, pp. 125–26.

16. Anton Chekhov, "The Black Monk," trans. Constance Garnett in *The Works of Anton Chekhov* (Roslyn, N.Y.: Black's, 1929), pp. 65–88.

17. William Carlos Williams, *Imaginations* (New York: New Directions, 1971), p. 135.

18. Italo Calvino, "Myth in the Narrative," trans. Erica Freiberg in *Surfiction: Fiction Now and Tomorrow*, ed. Raymond Federman (Chicago: Swallow, 1975), p. 79.

Robert Coover on His Own and Other Fictions: An Interview

Larry McCaffery
San Diego State University

Robert Coover didn't want to do the interview that follows. The 70's were a difficult period for Bob, both personally and creatively, mostly due to the enormous hassles and frustrations he suffered in connection with getting *The Public Burning* published. Having devoted nearly ten years and a great deal of his creative energies to the writing of *The Public Burning*, it developed that he also lost quite a stretch of writing time in trying to see the work through to its publication. At any rate, he was understandably reluctant to tie up any more of his writing-time when I would occasionaly bring up the possibility of an interview during several years of correspondence. Finally, though, he relented, and I flew to Providence, Rhode Island, where he had recently moved following almost fifteen years of living in England and Spain. The following interview took place on November 15, 1979, with a few minor follow-up questions being handled by mail.

Robert Coover is one of the most intense literary figures anyone is likely to encounter. After an evening of drinking wine and exchanging anecdotes at his house with his close friends, Robert Scholes, Jack Hawkes and their wives, we met for our interview at the lounge of the ancient Brown University English Department. Bob then led the way through the labyrinthine corridors of this building to an unobtrusive, unmarked door which he uses to work in. Coover is a rather short, slightly built man with thick brown hair and a quick, boyish smile that makes him look fifteen years younger than his forty-eight years. In answering questions, he spoke with passionate and confident conviction; although he chose his words carefully, Coover expressed his opinions forcefully. All around us—on his desk, walls, even the floor—were note cards and manuscript pages, written in different colored inks, from his various works in progress.

Coover is the author of three novels: *The Origin of the Brunists* (1966), which won the William Faulkner Award for the best first novel by an American author; *The Universal Baseball Association* (1968); and *The Public Burning* (1977). His short fiction includes one collection, *Pricksongs and Descants* (1969), and the recent publication of two novellas, *Charlies in the House of Rue* and *Spanking the Maid* (both published in 1980). He has also written a series of plays, collected in *A Theological Position* (1972). He is currently at work on several projects, including a major novel tentatively titled *Lucky Pierre*.

An Interview with Robert Coover

McCAFFERY: You've done most of your writing during the past ten or fifteen years while living in England and Spain. Are there any advantages to being an expatriate writer?

COOVER: Detachment mainly. A writer needs isolation, a cell of his own, that's obvious, but distance can also help. It has a way of freeing the imagination, stirring memory. Fewer localisms creep in, less passing trivia, transient concerns. Personally, I don't seem to be able to cut myself off very well here in the States. I get too engaged in things around me and end up having less time to write, less energy for it. It can work both ways of course. If you're not careful you can stay away too long and lose touch. No easy answer.

M: You say in your "Introduction" to the Fiction Collective's *Statements Two* that "in America, art, like everything else (knowledge, condoms, religions, etc.) is a product. The discovery of this is the capstone to the artist's alienation process in America." I take it from this that you feel that the commodity-mentality of American culture makes it even more difficult to be an artist in America than it is elsewhere—in Europe, for example.

C: Yes—in fact, many Europeans have been shocked at their own transformation when they enter the American market. Of course, art's treated as a commodity throughout most of the Western World—and elsewhere, maybe even worse—but in America the market's so vast and impersonal. To most Americans the publishing industry is as strange and remote as Oz, but it's also true the other way around: to the industry, the American public is like a magical and unpredictable fairyland, "out there somewhere," complete with a fabulous buried treasure just waiting to be dug up. There is no common language or concerns between them; their only exchange is barter. A writer exists as a kind of icon, or else as nothing. If this, or something like it, happened to a writer in Europe, he would at least have his own intellectual community to fall back on. Here we have no such communities—nor is there any real hope for one. There's no place for it, no physical way to work it out. The nearest thing we have is the academic circuit, where the steady flow of jobs, readings, conferences, visiting lectureships, and so on, bring people together, but it's very loosely strung, and many people have no access to it. And besides, it's been drying up. We have no gathering places, no forum, no national magazines, no cafes, no boulevards. We do not get together and talk about things on national TV or radio. P.E.N. is trying to do something about it now, setting up local chapters, but the effort is necessarily full of artifice—a kind of thinking man's Rotary Club: we have no natural center.

M: The Fiction Collective also seems to be trying to do what they can to change things—what do you think of their efforts to date?

C: Well, it also has to compete in the marketplace. It doesn't have much time for anything else. And its people are scattered and they lack the money for getting everybody together. It should be a more exciting phenomenon than it is, but it's still largely a publishing maneuver. As such, though, important. Probably, overall, they've put out the best list in town.

M: On the other hand, you've also said that you feel there's not much life in the fiction coming out of Europe today; yet American fiction, from my vantage point, has been enormously exciting during the sixties and seventies. Doesn't this seem contradictory to you?

C: No. A writer may or may not be discouraged by isolation and alienation. If he goes on, he may even benefit from it. Highly communalized groups of intellectuals like you have in Europe probably put more pressure on their members to conform to certain standards, discouraging too much eccentricity or adventurism. The standards are probably higher, though, letting less shit through. It's like going to a very good school: you must learn what's being taught at that school rather than striking out on your own. You gain discipline, knowledge, historical perspective, and so on, but you may lose a little confidence in your own imaginative potential. Besides, we may have been underestimating the quality of European fiction during this period when writing in the Americas seemed to be enjoying such a renaissance. After all, not only are there all the masters of the old forms, there are writers like Tournier and Beckett and Grass, Calvino, Carter,

Gombrowicz, and so on. Perhaps we've also had an exaggerated notion
of our own uniqueness and importance and quality. Novelty can hide a
lot of flaws.

M: But this renaissance you speak of—you've suggested that most
of the important contemporary American writers weren't even aware of
each other's works: so what was going on to generate this creative
outburst?

C: Well, many reasons probably. The postwar appetite for change
and newness, the college boom and the money that was around—all
those new English professors, for example, needing something to write
about—and then little things like the Kafka phenomenon, Barney
Rosset's Grove Press and the new paperback industry, the resurgence of
interest in the surrealists, ease of travel, the explosion of all the new
media, video especially. And then there was the general feeling, especially during the Cold War, of being stifled by dogma, the sense that
so much of the trouble we found ourselves in was the consequence of
not being imaginative enough about the ways out. Plus the threat of
nuclear apocalypse: how could we go on thinking in the old trite ways
when every day we had to imagine the unimaginable? All the disci-
plines were affected, not just writing. Physics, for example, had long
since been leading the way. . . .

M: You mentioned the media. Obviously your fiction has been influenced by television, cinema and theater. Were you consciously
aiming at integrating elements from these other media?

C: I think in part it was unconscious. Stories tend to appear to me,
not as formal ideas, but as metaphors, and these metaphors seem to demand structures of their own: they seem to have an internal need for a
certain form. Nevertheless we've all been affected by film technology,
the information bombardment of television, and so on, and certainly
I've had a conscious desire to explore the ways all this makes our minds
work.

M: Can you say something more about these metaphors that your
fiction grows out of?

C: They're the germ, the thought, the image, the idea, out of
which all the rest grows. They're always a bit elusive, involving
thoughts, feelings, abstractions, visual material, all at once. I suppose
they're a little like dream fragments, in that such fragments always
contain, if you analyze them, so much more than at first you suspect.
But they're not literally that—I never write from dreams. All these

ideas come to me in the full light of day. Some, when you pry them open, have too little inside to work with. Others are unexpectedly fat and rich. Novels typically begin for me as very tiny stories or little one-act play ideas which I think at the time aren't going to fill three pages. Then slowly the hidden complexities reveal themselves.

M: Do you recall what this germinating idea was for *The Origin of the Brunists?*

C: Well, wholly fleshed out, of course, it's the book itself. But my first glimpse of it came one grim wintery day, just before Christmas, while I was sitting in the bleachers of a high school basketball gymnasium, eating a peanut-butter sandwich and staring down on five grotesquely burnt and mutilated cadavers. There had been a mine explosion, and I was there helping the guy who edited the newspaper my father managed, getting identifications and so on. They'd expected a steady flow of bodies, there were over a hundred men still below, but after they'd brought up the first five—this episode is sort of in the book—they decided to push on and see if they could find anyone still alive. So, for the moment, there was nothing for me to do but watch as relatives came in to try to identify these five almost unidentifiable men, all of which left me, as you can imagine, quite shaken. There was a lot of tearful praying going on, and it led me to wonder what might happen if some guy did get rescued, and came up thinking he'd been saved for some divine mission? What might that lead to? As a matter of fact, a man did get rescued, but though he was a religious man, he had no messianic complex, he was just thankful. Anyway, I carried this idea around for a while after that, experimenting with different approaches, but it wasn't until nearly ten years later, after a lot of the fictions in *Pricksongs* had been written, that I married this idea to the desire I was feeling then that I wanted to pay my dues, as it were, to traditional fiction. The germinating idea, of course, was by now a folder full of elaborate notes, half-starts, experimental inventions, and so on, but no matter what the variations, they always had something to do with a coal mine disaster, and it was this, more than the messiah story, that now made me want to try this story as a full-length mimetic fiction. In effect, I wanted to go down into the mine myself and come out of it, hopefully with some revelations of my own, new insights, more skill, discipline, all that. And that was pretty much how it turned out. It was a very valuable experience for me.

M: But if you're "paying your dues" to traditional narrative approaches in *The Origin of the Brunists*, I sometimes sense that you're paying them with reservations; there seem to be a very large amount of non-realistic elements in the novel, at least on certain levels. Did you really conceive the novel to be a straightforward realistic presentation?

C: Yes, it is, of course. Maybe I think that all my fiction is realistic and that so far it has simply been misunderstood as otherwise. There are paradoxes of course. Though the varying perspectives may at times seem to disturb the "realism" of the book, the overview that embraces them all I think is wholly realistic—and yet this overview includes the book's design, and that design is born of, well, something else. That vibrant space between the poles of a paradox: that's where all the exciting art happens, I think.

M: In the *Brunists*—and in your other novels as well—one of your main thematic intentions seems to be to expose the so-called "objective reports" of history, news reporting, theological dictums, and so forth; you suggest that such reports result largely from man's desire to shape random events into some kind of pleasing pattern or design. Do you mean to suggest that all these spring from a central artistic impulse?

C: I wouldn't say "artistic." Art's not nature after all. But, yes, the human need for pattern, and language's propensity, willy nilly, for supplying it—what happens, I think, is that every effort to form a view of the world, every effort to speak of the world, involves a kind of fiction-making process. Memory is a kind of narrative, as is our perception of what the future is apt to bring us, our understanding of anything going on out in the world—even our scientific understanding of the world has to be reduced to a narrative of sorts in order to grasp it. What's a formula but a kind of sentence, a story among other possible stories? Men live by fictions. They have to. Life's too complicated, we just can't handle all the input, we have to isolate little bits and make reasonable stories out of them. Of course, that's an artificial act and therefore, you might say, "artistic." But I would say the impulse was from necessity, and only some of the resulting stories are "artistic." All of them, though, are merely artifices—that is, they are always in some ways false, or at best incomplete. There are always other plots, other settings, other interpretations. So if some stories start throwing their weight around, I like to undermine their authority a bit, work variations, call attention to their fictional natures.

M: Is this your explanation as to why we have had this outburst of self-reflective fictions during the sixties and seventies?

C: Yes. If story-telling is central to the human experience, stories about story-telling, or stories which talk about themselves as stories, become central too. For awhile anyway. I think, as a fashion, it's passing, though more self-reflective fictions will be written.

M: One of the frequent criticisms leveled against metafiction is that by concentrating on the act of writing, by becoming more involuted and self-conscious, it becomes narcissistic and evades the kind of "moral issues" that John Gardner has recently championed. Do you feel there is an inherent opposition between didactic and aesthetic aims in a work of fiction?

C: No, it's a phony issue. John's a moral fiction-writer—some of the time, probably not often enough—but he's an immoral moralist. He knows this debate about "entertainment" and "instruction" is a terribly old, seedy issue, a kind of political game at its worst, that goes back to the ancients. Who's to say, for example, that self-reflective fiction, dealing as it assumes it does with a basic human activity, is not, by examining that activity as it celebrates it, engaged in a very moral act?

M: But you wouldn't insist that good fiction must be moral in the way that Gardner suggests it must—that is, by creating heroic models, proposing solutions to issues rather than simply raising them, or whatever?

C: I would not, myself, say that fiction *must* anything. Ever.

M: I find your fiction repeatedly returning to a central situation: we observe a character or characters engaged in this subjective, fiction-making process we have just been talking about; in their desire for stability and order, however, they lose sight of what they have been doing and begin to insert these fictions into the world as dogma; this winds up entrapping or even destroying them. Is this a fair reading?

C: Yes, why not?

M: Why do you return so often to this idea?

C: To the scene of the crime, you mean? A weakness no doubt, a lack of moral fiber. Maybe the struggle I had as a young writer against the old forms made me overly aware of their restrictive nature, such that I found myself burdened with a vast number of metaphoric possibilities, all of which were touched by this sense of dogma invading the world and turning it to stone. But I have literally hundreds of ideas, virtually every day I think of another one, so maybe I'll get lucky next time, choose one with a different bloom. It's the choice that scares me.

I mean, we only have so many lives to lead. The *Brunists* took me four years, *The Public Burning* longer. If I could work through all the ideas I have now without thinking up any more (and as I said that, damn it, I've just thought of another one), I'd need a couple of hundred years more at least. Like human seed: a billion kids eager to be born every minute, but you only get a few at best, and probably not the ones you thought you wanted.

M: The first things you ever published were a series of poems in *The Fiddlehead*. Since then, you've worked with dramatic forms, movie scripts, translation, and various other literary forms. Which ones have you found the most interesting to work with and what are the most important differences among them?

C: The central thing for me is story. I like poems, paintings, music, even buildings, that tell stories. I believe, to be good, you have to master the materials of the form you're working in, whether it's language, form and color, meter, stone, cameras, lights, or inks, but all that's secondary to me. Necessary but secondary. I know there's a way of looking at fiction as being made up of words and that therefore what you do with words becomes the central concern, but I'm much more interested in the way that fiction, for all its weaknesses, reflects something else—gesture, connections, paradox, story. I work with language because paper is cheaper than film stock. And because it's easier to work with a committee of one. But storytelling doesn't have to be done with words on a printed page, or even with spoken words: we all learned that as kids at our Saturday morning religious experience in the local ten-cent cinemas. Probably, if I had absolute freedom to do what I want, I'd prefer film.

M: What is it that excites you so much about film?

C: First of all, its great immediacy: it grasps so much with such rapidity. Certainly, it's the medium *par excellence* for the mimetic narrative. And it has a relationship with time that is fascinating: we can take in centuries in an hour or two, even in a few minutes. All narratives play with time, but only film can truly juggle it. So: a mix of magic and documentary power. And I don't dislike the communal aspect of film, the bringing together of a lot of different talents to produce a work of art—it's healthier somehow than that deep closeted ego-involvement of the novelist, poet, or painter. But the problem of course is that it's so expensive and potentially so profitable: too many non-creative types get in on the processes, more than one good film's been ruined by them. The tales of woe from writers misused by the film industry are beyond number.

M: What about your experiences with the theater?

C: Like film, it's terribly destructive of creative time. You find yourself working long hours over five or six lines that took you maybe fifteen minutes to write. And before that there's the casting, the designing of the set, struggles with producers and directors, costumes, music maybe—and if you're going to get seriously involved with theater, you've got to get involved with all of it. But there's something exhilarating about it too—it's a kind of Pygmalion experience, seeing it come alive before your eyes. And all the performing arts have the excitement of ephemerality. Novelists sometimes get this sense of the weightiness of their task, as though they were chipping their work out on stone—one slip and it's all ruined forever. Contrarily, every night at the theater it's all brand new—and when it's over, it's gone, except as it exists in memory, so long as that lasts. It gives me a sense of living in the present that I rarely get as a novelist.

M: Have you ever gotten involved in the productions of your plays?

C: Yes, several times, most intensely a few years ago in the New York production of "The Kid" at the American Place Theatre. Jack Gelber was the director, and working with him and with Wynn Handman who ran the theater was one of the happiest experiences in my life. We made a mistake in the casting which proved to be troublesome and there were a few decisions made that maybe weren't wise ones, but there's always going to be this—if we did it again, there would be others, that's part of the fun of it. For the most part, it was a wonderful show, greatly enhanced by all the talents that contributed to it. Jack got an Obie for directing it and the production won several other awards. It was a real treat. I was also very modestly involved in a wonderful production of "Love Scene" in Paris, where it premiered, there called "Scene d'Amour." It was directed by Henri Gilabert in a little Left Bank theater called the Troglodyte and with such intelligence and balance that it was like seeing before my eyes—and in French at that—exactly what I'd envisioned in my mind before. "Rip Awake" premiered out in Los Angeles where Ron Sossi played Rip, and his Odyssey group also premiered "A Theological Position."

M: I'm sure you heard of the scandal that surrounded "A Theological Position"'s production out here.

C: Yes. Well, Ron probably asked for it by including it in what he called "An Evening of Dirty Religious Plays," but my work's had a long history of suppression, of bowdlerization, so I'm used to it. Actually, I don't see it as a scandalous play—there's nothing new about talking cunts, after all. Probably, for some of the people on the council out there, the image struck too close to home. Anyway, it's a good theater group, and I hope to work more with them.

M: Those Western materials you used in "The Kid" you've also used in other stories, and you return repeatedly to fairy tales, sports, and other elements that are usually seen as pop-cultural material. What's the source of your fascination with this kind of stuff?

C: It's all material that's close to the mythic content of our lives, and is therefore an important part of our day-to-day fiction-making process. The pop-culture we absorb in childhood—and I'd include all the pop-religions as well—goes on affecting the way we respond to the world or talk about it for the rest of our lives. And this mythology of ours, this unwritten Bible, is being constantly reinforced by books and newspapers, films, television, advertisements, politicians, teachers, and so on. So working inside these forms is a way of staying close to the bone.

M: What about your interest in another concept that recurs in your fiction—the concept of number and its inevitable companion, numerology? These both seem to be a perfect example of what you described earlier as fictions man uses to navigate through the world.

C: Yes, or to stumble through it. It's one way among many that the mind gets locked into fixed distorting patterns. Silly stuff. But it was an important element in the Christian apocalyptic vision, so it had to be part of the *Brunists*. Then, once I started working with it, I found it useful in a lot of secondary and ironic ways. Especially in the formal design.

M: You mean like Calvino's use of Tarot images in *The Castle of Crossed Destinies*? He seems to be using Tarot in that book as a generating formal design in much the same way that you use number theory in a story like "The Elevator."

C: Mmm. Tarot exists in the *Brunists* too. You remember the widows of the miners gathered at Mabel's and sat around her cards in the key chapter of the section called "The Sign." It's also in the structure. Number presents itself more directly, you recognize it more quickly.

M: What about your apparent interest in puns and word-play?

Freud maintains that one derives pleasure from the pun or the play on words by following the possibilities and transformations implicit in language. Gombrich describes this process as: "The juxtaposition of concepts which one arrives at casually, unexpectedly, unleashes a pre-conscious idea." Does your fascination with puns have to do with this view of the transformational possibilities lying within the formal properties of language?

C: I was more fascinated just now with the Gombrich quote. It's a painterly thought: the shock of strange juxtapositions. I like the pun for its intense condensation, but for me it's only a second-rate version of the more exciting idea of the juxtaposition of two unexpected elements—structural puns, you might call them. A lot of my stories begin this way. Again the use of seeming paradox, the vibrant space between the poles.

M: Is that how "The Panel Game" got started? It's obviously very much concerned with this business of word play.

C: Yes, but it's an early breakaway story for me, so it's more self-conscious than most. I was struggling to do something I had never done before, and it shows. All seven of the stories in that little "Exemplary Fictions" section of *Pricksongs* are discovery stories like that, blind launchings-forth as it were. I only selected those that seemed unique turning-points. Thus, "The Panel Game" is a mid-1950's story and the next one in that group is already from the 1960's with a lot missing in between.

M: You wrote me once that "The Panel Game" was an important early story for you, and when I looked back at it, it seemed to contain the seeds of a lot of the central motifs in your later work—the struggle with transformation, the attempt to unravel a structure encoded in symbols, the game metaphor, and so on.

C: Yes, well, Borges said we go on writing the same story all our lives. The trouble is, it's usually a story that can never be told—there's always this distance between the sign and the signified, it's the oldest truth in philosophy—and that's why we tend to get so obsessive about it. The important thing is to accept this unbridgeable distance, and carry on with the crazy bridge-building just the same.

M: In *The Origin of the Brunists* you say that "games were what kept Tiger Miller going." The same is obviously true of Henry Waugh in *The Universal Baseball Association* and, in a different sense, of Richard Nixon in *The Public Burning* as well. Why do you return so often to this concept of game in your fiction?

C: We live in a skeptical age in which games are increasingly important. When life has no ontological meaning, it becomes a kind of game itself. Thus it's a kind of metaphor for a perception of the way the world works, and also something that almost everybody's doing. If not on the playing fields, then in politics or business or education. If you're cynical about it, you learn the rules and strategies, shut up about them, and get what you can out of it. If you're not inclined to be a manipulator, you might want to expose the game-plan for your own protection and ask how it can be a better game than it is at present. And formal games reflect on the hidden games, more so in an age without a Final Arbiter. So it's an important metaphor to be explored.

M: The game of writing not to be excepted, I assume. I mean, Henry's relationship with his baseball association seems to share a number of interesting parallels with the way a writer relates to a novel, and I believe you've said somewhere that you intended the book to be primarily for writers rather than for baseball fans. Do you mean that you intended the book to be a sort of allegory of the writer's plight or situation?

C: That statement had to do with the fact that when I was working on that particular book I was convinced that it had no audience—it had become too eccentric an idea. But I felt that imbedded in it were a lot of ideas, notions about fiction and about the activity of the imagination itself, its role in the world, the interplay of formal and informal fictions, and so on. And I thought that, if no one else did, at least other writers would perceive this, would see what I was doing and would be fascinated by how I worked out my problems. Seeing the way a little metaphor slipped through here and there, working its way out, they'd receive a kind of greeting, a recognition, a signal. Of course, it turned out somewhat differently. The book has had an unexpectedly large readership. It turned out to be popular among athletes and other people involved in sports, journalists especially. And, as it happens, there are a lot more people playing table-top baseball games than I could ever have imagined.

M: Once and for all, would you clear up exactly where Henry is in the last chapter?

C: No.

M: Okay, okay, leave that a mystery if you must, I only asked because my students always ask me the question. . . . But it's one of my favorite chapters, and one of the things you seem to be doing is playfully tearing down some of the mythic and religious parallels you had been establishing earlier in the novel.

C: Well, in that sense it might be seen as a gift to the unobservant reader who had taken those parallels too seriously in the first place. I believe it reinforces the central themes of the book, bringing it all into focus without at the same time turning it off.

M: Keeping things open-ended, you mean—is that one of the reasons that your last chapter is the *eighth* chapter, rather than the ninth which we might have expected in keeping with your baseball metaphor?

C: Yes, the design, the structure of the book is so self-revealing—and it's not a gloss on the text from which it borrows its design, in the sense of being a theologian's gloss; it's an outsider's gloss, an ironist's gloss. The idea of an "eighth" chapter, the potential of it, the wonderful ambivalences implied, all this came to me even before I knew what was going to be in it.

M: Part of what's in it I seem to see in all three of your novels: a crowd coming together and in the interactions producing a significant collective response of some sort. Am I right in seeing Durkheim's influence here?

M: Yes, especially his image of "collective effervescence," which is his explanation, in part, for the invention of divinities.

M: Certainly, it's important to *The Public Burning* as well.

C: Yes—where would Uncle Sam be without it?

M: And that whole final section there, that "dream time" experience as you call it—is that notion from the same source?

C: No, it's a primitive expression, but I first read about it in the works of a French writer named Roger Caillois. "Dream time" is a ritual return to the mythic roots of a group of people. A tribe might set aside a time every year to do this, most often during initiation rites—to take the young who are coming into the tribe as adults and deliver them into an experience in which they relive the experiences of the civilizing heroes. If you go back to dream time, of course, you must first pretend that the tribe has not yet been civilized, that the rules you live by have not yet come into existence. So everything gets turned upside down, all the rules are upended, and then, through the mythic experiences of the civilizing hero, you recreate the society and discover your place in it. It usually involves dope, mock-battles, sexual initiation, scarring, and so on, and is a very awesome and exciting experience, with the whole tribe involved. This idea of a ritual bath of prehistoric or preconscious experience was very attractive to me as I began developing the Rosenberg book, not merely for its contributions to the final section, but also because I realized that this was one of the great disruptive functions of art: to take the tribe back into dream time, pulling them in, letting them relive their preconscious life as formed for them by their tribe. So, though its function is more obvious at the end of the book, it is hopefully operative throughout. I think, for example, that many of the people who have remarked on the way they empathized with Nixon were, in fact, having this kind of experience. They were finding their way back to the formative elements of themselves that they had not suspected or questioned before.

M: Yes, critics and reviewers have often remarked on this surprising empathy they feel for Nixon. How did you happen to choose him to be your central narrator in *The Public Burning*?

C: I'm not sure whether it was a matter of choice or necessity—he emerged from the texts, as it were. He has a way of doing that, fighting his way to the center stage, it's hard to stop him. Nevertheless, there were other possibilities. The book began as a little theater idea, which grew into a series of rather raucous circus acts. I began to feel the need for a quieter voice to break in from time to time. I wanted someone who lived inside the mythology, accepting it, and close to the center, yet not quite in the center, off to the edge a bit, an observor. A number of characters auditioned for the part, but Nixon, when he appeared, proved ideal.

M: Why was that?

C: Well, for one thing he's such a self-conscious character. He has to analyze everything, work out all the parameters, he worries about things—and then there's his somewhat suspicious view of the world. He doesn't trust people very much—often for good reason. He lives in a world where trust is often misplaced, and he learned early to trust no one. And that included Eisenhower, J. Edgar Hoover, the whole government and judicial establishment. And this attitude of his allowed me to reach skeptical conclusions through him about what was happening at the time of the Rosenberg executions, which would have been difficult from other viewpoints. For Eisenhower, if the FBI and the courts said so, then the Rosenbergs were guilty, they had to be, but Nixon could doubt this. He could imagine that his best ally, a man like Hoover, say, might not be letting him see everything. He could see the case in terms of who stood to gain what from it. And, of course, I also had it on faith from the beginning that any exploration of Nixon, this man who has played such a large role in American society since World War II, would have to reveal something about us all. It was another quality,though, that first called him forth in my mind—this was in 1969, just after he'd been elected President—and that was his peculiar talent for making a fool of himself.

M: You've spoken of seeing him as a kind of clown. . . .

C: Yes. I was developing this series of circus acts—all these verbal acrobatics, death-defying highwire acts, showy parades, and so on—and I needed a clown to break in from time to time and do a few pratfalls. He was perfect for this. For a while anyway. Eventually his real-life pratfalls nearly undid my own. I couldn't keep up with him. Had I been able to finish the book in time to publish it in 1972—as a kind of election-year gift to the incumbent, as it were—life would have been a lot easier. On the other hand, the Watergate episode forced me to work a lot harder, dig deeper, think beyond the pratfalls. So I probably ended up with a better book. Dearly as it cost me.

M: Your novella, "Whatever Happened to Gloomy Gus of the Chicago Bears," appeared in the *American Review* during this period when you were working on *The Public Burning* and it also deals with Nixon. Was it originally conceived to be an integral part of your bigger project?

C: No, it was completely separate, though there is a writerly connection, in that I used it to work off some of my frustrations with *The Public Burning*. One of the peculiarities of *The Public Burning* was that it was made up of thousands and thousands of tiny fragments that had to be painstakingly stitched together, and it was not hard to lose patience with it. It was like a gigantic impossible puzzle. I was striving for a text that would seem to have been written by the whole nation through all its history, as though the sentences had been forming themselves all this time, accumulating toward this experience—I wanted thousands of echoes, all the sounds of the nation. Well, the idea was good, but the procedures were sometimes unbelievably tedious. And at some low point, I got a request from a popular magazine for a sports story. That's what happens when you write a book with "baseball" in the title. I turned them down, of course, but the idea stuck in my head somewhere and niggled at me. One of the many successful failures in Nixon's life had been his abortive high school and college football career, but I hadn't found much space for it in *The Public Burning*. In an idle moment, I married this to his belief that if you just work hard enough at something you could achieve it, and considered an alternate career for him as a pro football player. As this would have had to have taken place in the 1930's, it suddenly opened up for me the possibility of writing a good old-fashioned 1930's-style novella, full of personal material, thoughtful asides and so on. Everything fell into place like magic and I sat down at the machine and for the first time in years just banged happily away. It was the most joyful writing experience I ever had. It was very refreshing and probably helped me get on through to the end of *The Public Burning*.

M: There must have been some moments when you felt you'd never finish *The Public Burning*. . . .

C: Oh yes, many times. The worst moment was probably when Hal Scharlatt, my editor at Dutton, died. Hal was man with a lot of strengths and he was very supportive. He was the only man, I felt, who would ever publish this book. And he was a friend. When he died suddenly, a young man still, I went through a very sorrowful time. It was as though all the props had been pulled out from under this monstrous thing I was building, and I was about to be flattened by it. I no longer believed it would be published, and had to write against this certainty. And I was very nearly right.

M: Your problems in getting the book published after you finished it are already nearly legendary. What happened, from your perspective?

C: It's a complicated story, but at its heart is a betrayal by my editor at Knopf, Bob Gottlieb, who failed to stand by me or the book when it counted, and so it cost me a lot of harassment and a couple of years of my writing life. The book was finished in 1975 and that summer, with a lot of seeming enthusiasm, Gottlieb wrested the manuscript away from Dutton, promising to publish it in 1976 during the Bicentennial and the Presidential elections. I was living in England at the time and made a trip back to the States at my own expense that autumn in order to complete the editing with Gottlieb and with Ted Solotaroff of Bantam, the company involved in the paperback rights. But then, with the book going into production just after Christmas, the RCA and Random House corporation lawyers began putting pressure on Knopf, and Gottlieb soon knuckled under, even suggesting to me on the phone that the book might be after all "immoral." I understand that the final decision to suppress the book came from the Random House boss Bob Bernstein, who shortly thereafter won a Freedom of the Press award. The book went from house to house then amid a lot of false rumors, getting rejected by one set of corporation lawyers after another. I finally had to return to the States myself to sort it out, though by then I'd already lost over a year, the Bicentennial which might have cushioned its publication had passed, and the book had become a kind of notorious hot potato. Eventually Richard Seaver convinced Viking to do the book. There were a lot of conditions. They refused to pay off Knopf, for example, on the reasonable grounds that Knopf had broken their contract with me and were owed nothing—indeed, they had even made it more difficult to get the book published successfully. Viking also held all my moneys due in escrow for several years in case of legal costs, for which they held me 100% responsible. At the same time, the house lawyers did everything they could to pressure me to emasculate the book, though in the end, thanks mainly to Dick Seaver with support from Tom Guinzburg, the book did go through and was given a good production. As for Knopf, they still held Bantam tied to the old contract and refused to let them go—and thus, in effect, since Bantam's support was the key to Viking's willingness to do the book, refused to let the book be published at all—until I signed a separate statement saying that I owed them all advances paid, and I am still paying off the debt today. Finally, two and a half totally disruptive years after I had finished it, the book appeared.

M: Did this legal situation which developed have any direct effect on your aesthetic decisions about the book—say, in the final editing process?

C: No. There were a lot of unpleasant pressures, but they were resisted. Dick Seaver was a big help in this, acting as a buffer against the worst of it. Both he and Solotaroff were very helpful editors, two of the few good editors left in the industry. The book needed cutting and we worked hard to do this, taking out maybe a quarter of the original manuscript. Dealing with lawyers at the new house Viking was much worse, we had some bad sessions, and I became very tenacious finally, anxious to hang on to everything in fear that I was being asked for the wrong reasons to take it out. The book's probably still informed a bit by that anxious tenacity.

M: As you were developing the book, did you see your role as being, in any way, a vindicator of the Rosenbergs? I say this because it seemed pretty evident to me in reading the book that you felt the Rosenbergs were, if not completely innocent, then certainly not guilty enough to justify being executed.

C: I originally felt back in 1966 that the execution of the Rosenbergs had been a watershed event in American history which we had somehow managed to forget or repress. I felt it was important to resurrect it and look at it again. By the time I'd finished researching the thing I was convinced, one, that they were not guilty as charged, and, two, even had they been, the punishment was hysterical and excessive. Indeed, given the macho arrogance of our military establishment, if anyone did contribute to the proliferation of information about the bomb, they probably did us all a favor. They were dead, there was no one to feel sorry for, I wasn't trying to vindicate them in that sense, but it was important that we remember it, that we not be so callous as to just shrug it off, or else it can happen again and again.

M: Various reviewers used the term "apocalyptic" in describing the mood of this book. Is that accurate?

C: No. Apocalypse is a magical idea borrowed from Christian mythology and the notion of cyclical time and a purpose in history. But short of apocalypse, there's always disaster, which we have visited upon us from day to day. We have had, in that sense, an unending sequence of apocalypses, long before Christianity began and up to the present. From generation to generation, whole peoples get wiped from the face of the earth, so for them the apocalypse has already happened. And we can be pretty sure there's more to come. I mean, who can stop it? And technologically it's so much more frightening today. So, in a lot of contemporary fiction, there's a sense of boding disaster which is part of the times, just like self-reflective fictions.

M: Let's talk about what you are working on right now. When I met you seven or eight years ago, you were working on a long book called *Lucky Pierre*, which you were very excited about. Are you still engaged in that project?

C: Yes, but other things have intervened. I've been working on theater pieces, radio plays, things like that. And shorter fictions. After the gigantism of *The Public Burning*, this is the year of the small book. Five of them, in fact. Viking is publishing one of then, *A Political Fable*, which originally appeared in 1968 as "The Cat in the Hat for President," and the other four are being done by small presses. Two of them are in the form of filmscripts, written nearly twenty years ago. The other two are new novella-length fictions, *Charlie in the House of Rue*, from Penmaen Press, and *Spanking the Maid*, which Bruccoli-Clark is publishing. And there's another novel-length fiction, not too long I hope, which is on my desk and walls right now, so Lucky Pierre will have to wait yet a bit longer. Impatient as he is, the restless fucker.

Daniel Martin and the Mimetic Task

Robert Alter
University of California, Berkeley

John Fowles, in an age too artistically dispersed to have contemporary models for emulation, has managed to make himself something of an exemplary novelist. His fiction, that is, whatever its limitations, repeatedly points in variously interesting ways to the possibilities and problematics of the novel as an instrument for the apprehension of reality. Writing, moreover, after Joyce and Proust, after the *Nouveau Roman*, and now after Structuralism, Fowles has been impelled to make his novels not only illustrative in their mimetic acts but also formally investigative, fashioned as self-conscious artifices that inquire, sometimes with discursive explicitness, into the nature of fiction and the kinds of access it may give us to extra-literary experience. At his best, he can be the most instructive of living English novelists.

Daniel Martin (1977) is the longest and most ambitious of Fowles's novels, and it has some suggestive things to tells us about why the novel as a genre continues to excite the imagination of both serious writers and readers in this last quarter of the twentieth century. It is a book with certain large resonances, which I would like to consider, though I don't mean to propose it as a contemporary masterpiece. If novels of the 1970s are still read a hundred years from now, I imagine it will not seem to be our *Middlemarch* but rather a *Daniel Deronda* or perhaps no more than a *Felix Holt the Radical* of our age. Even that degree of achievement, however, should be amply sufficient to warrant critical attention, and may provide some indication of what the novel now is capable of doing. Since I do not intend to investigate the book's flaws, let me simply mention the principal ones before setting them aside: a palpable tendency to run on too long about the same fictional matters, and an occasional weakness for indulging easy fantasy instead of inventing persuasive fiction (as, for example, in Daniel Martin's brief, supposedly idyllic ménage with two utterly simple and honest,

utterly compliant working-class sisters). Such self-indulgence is fortu-
nately infrequent, and the *longueurs*, particularly perceptible in the extended dialogues, occur for the most part in the first half of the novel,
before the protagonist begins to fix on the object of his quest and sets
out in pursuit of it. The quest itself is finally what will engage our attention here, but first we must have some sense of the formal and cir-
cumstantial contexts which the novel establishes for it.

Daniel Martin, one may recall, is a successful British film writer
who, by the necessity of his profession, sojourns a good deal of the time
in Los Angeles, where he is seen at the beginning of the main action
living in mutual though rather disoriented affection with a Scottish actress half his age. The first impetus of transition in the plot is to get
Dan back to London and ultimately back to the Devon village of his
childhood, which is to say, back to himself and to his formative experiences. This transition is suddenly effected through a death-bed summons from Anthony Mallory, Dan's best friend from his university
years at Oxford after the Second World War, who has been totally es-
tranged from him for a decade and a half. Dan flies back to England,
rushes to Anthony's hospital at Oxford, and the two men are reconciled. Later that evening, Anthony, having thus settled the chief out-
standing account in his life, anticipates the cancer that is killing him
by jumping out the window and thus leaving Dan, in all ambiguous
senses of the verb, with his wife Jane.

Fowles, for thematic purposes that will become apparent, deliberately convolutes the relationships of the principal characters: Jane is the
sister of Dan's ex-wife; during the period of the two sisters' respective
engagements to Anthony and Dan at Oxford, there was a suggestion
that there existed a deeper affinity between Jane and Dan than between
either sister and her actual fiancé; and in a crucial scene in the earliest
of the novel's flashbacks to the young adult Dan, Jane, who has been
prenuptually chaste with Anthony, peremptorily offers herself to Dan.
This single sexual joining is undertaken, in those years of the vogue of
Existentialism, as an *acte gratuit*, but the partners to it will eventually
discover that it was something else in fact. Now, the newly widowed
Jane is persuaded, after considerable resistance, to accompany Daniel
Martin on a tour of Egypt, purely on a basis of comfortable companion-
ship between middle-aged friends. In the course of this trip, which is
the last major sequence of action in the novel, Dan rather unexpectedly
comes to a realization of what he needed to be looking for all along.

The entire story is told, moreover, in ways which reflect the novelist's constant awareness that to tell any such story, whether it is pure invention or, as one may surmise, somehow a refraction of the novelist's own life-experience, requires a continuous manipulation of artifice, a continuous tacking between the various pressures of literary form and convention and the demand or aspiration of fidelity to experience. Early on, Dan raises the prospect of putting aside his film scripts to attempt a novel, and from the end of the first chapter, the narrative cuts back and forth between first person and the third person in which it began, alternately allowing Dan to recollect his own experience in his own voice and setting him at a distance as a fictional personage distinct from the narrator. Or is this narrator, we begin to wonder, not the autonomous "authorial" agency we at first assumed but rather a fictional construct, a formal strategem invented by the character Daniel Martin for the clearer rendering of his own experience in a novelistic narrative? The novel Dan intends to write but never will, we are told in the very last sentence of the book, "can never be read, lies eternally in the future, his ill-concealed ghost has made that impossible last [sentence] his own impossible first." The novel John Fowles has written thus opens up at the end (instead of "concluding") in a shimmer of ambiguity about its own status. The most likely candidate for "the ill-concealed ghost" is of course Fowles himself, standing behind the would-be novelist Daniel Martin, projecting him out of the stuff of his, the real writer's, experience, using that unmentioned last sentence of the fictional character as the motto and first sentence of the novel we have just read: "WHOLE SIGHT; OR ALL THE REST IS DESOLATION." Actually to have reproduced that sentence at the end would have given the book too much formal closure: it is a brave ideal to which everything in the novel aspires, but which Fowles does not want to claim resoundingly as an accomplished fact, and so the sentence is an "impossible" one, imposing an imperative of complete vision that may not be realizable. In order to understand better what is implied by whole sight, we shall now have to get a clearer view of the novel's determined and sometimes polemic approach to mimesis.

Daniel Martin begins with a chapter entitled "The Harvest"—and of course, the distinctly uncontemporary practice of using chapter-titles is itself a means of flaunting artifice—which is a virtuoso performance of descriptive writing. It will not be evident, however, until much later in the book what purpose is served by the virtuosity. The harvesting goes on against the temporal backdrop of the early days of the war, with some apprehensiveness on the part of the laboring Devon farmers that German planes may at any moment darken the bright August sky. The boy Daniel Martin is a participant and an observer in the scene, as one of the rural crowd, but he does not yet clearly emerge as a discriminated central character—that will occur only in the second chapter, the first of the Oxford episodes. Here is a characteristic moment in "The Harvest":

> They all gather round the last piece: stookers, children, old men, Babe and his lurcher: a black-and-liver dog with a cowed, much-beaten look, always crouched, neurotic, hyperalert and Argus-eyed, never a yard from his master's heels. The young woman walks up on swollen ankles, carrying her baby son in her arms, the pram left by the gate. Some have sticks, others pile stones. A ring of excited faces, scrutinizing each tremor in the rectangle of corn: commands, the older men knowing, sternly cautious. Doan'ee fuss, lad, keep back. In the rectangle's heart a stirring of ears, a ripple of shaken stems, like a trout-wave in a stream. A hen pheasant explodes with a rattling whir, brown-speckled jack-in-the-box, down the hill and over Fishacre Lane. Laughter. A small girl screams. A tiny rabbit, not eight inches long, runs out from the upper border, stops bemused, then runs again. The boy who helped stook stands ten yards away, grinning as a wild band of children sprawl and tumble after the tiny animal, which doubles, stops, spurts, and finally runs back into the wheat.[1]

The scene has no importance in the concatenation of the plot; it is not symbolic of anything; and the action reported—it will be followed by a general flushing-out and slaughter of rabbits by the villagers—is neither traumatic nor especially influential in its effect on the young Dan. Why, then, does Fowles take the time to do the scene in this detail and why does it engage our imagination as readers? The most notable characteristic of the passage, I would suggest, is what the narrator elsewhere, referring to an Oxford skit, calls "the decided and visible oomph of the mimesis" (p. 21). To begin with, a successful imitation of a familiar object through the expressive resources of written language is pleasurable both for the writer and the reader. The features of the passage that contribute to its mimetic effectiveness are evident enough. There is the gratuitous specification of detail, as in the new mother with her swollen ankles and her pram left at the gate, which helps produce what Roland Barthes has called *l'effet du réel*. This reinforces the sense of authority in the descriptive precision, which is felt visually in the rendering of the black-and-liver, much-beaten "lurcher" (a poacher's crossbred hunting-dog) at the beginning and quantitatively in the report of the baby rabbit, not eight inches long, at the end. Since the narrator renders his scene not with brush or camera but with words, he can choose ones that not only evoke the objects of description but interpret them, like the neurotic, hyperalert dog and the bemused rabbit, or that give them heightened intensity of presence through metaphor or allusion, like the Argus-eyes, the explosion of the pheasant as a brown-speckled jack-in-the-box, the likening of the rippling wheatfield to a trout-wave in a stream. Finally, the words are arranged in a syntactic-semantic sequence that mimics rhythmically the action represented, down to the tiny animal at the end that "doubles, stops, spurts, and finally runs back into the wheat."

All this is accomplished enough, though one might discover comparable descriptive performances in a dozen other well-written contemporary novels; but the question remains: what does this visible oomph of mimesis on the harvest field have to do with *Daniel Martin*? The real point of the scene, which we cannot yet realize eight pages into the novel because we do not yet know what the main temporal locus will be, is that it is something remembered. Daniel Martin's vocation as film writer will be thematically central because throughout the novel, film, as the dominant mimetic narrative art-form of our era, is used as a foil against which Fowles can show what the novel and the novel alone can do. The objects of representation of all novels are necessarily recollected objects, or to be more precise, recollected-and-reinvented objects. The novelist works with what happened to him yesterday, last month, or twenty years ago, not with what he can look up at and see as he sits at his desk. By contrast, cinematic objects of representation are always immediately present to the camera that records them instant by instant, frame by frame. The narrative order of past experience produced through this process is, Daniel Martin argues, fundamentally factitious: "All past shall be coeval, a backworld uniformly not present, relegated to the status of so many family snapshots. The mode of recollection usurps the reality of the recalled . . . , destroys the past of the mind of each spectator" (p. 87). One might in fact add that even films which try to deal imaginatively with the spell exercised by the past over the present, like Franco Brusati's remarkable *To Forget Venice* (1979), encounter serious formal problems, chiefly because of the tyranny of the cinematic flashback, however ingeniously modified, its tendency to create a literal equivalence among different times. Some film critics like to describe such films as "Proustian," but the very comparison suggests how primitive the visual medium remains in its access to the multilayered realm of recollection. Film, Daniel Martin the script writer is led to reflect on the contradictions of his own vocation, is "a constant flowing through nowness, . . . chained to the present image" (p. 331); and thus a violation of what he construes to be his own very English consciousness of living in an endless flurry of multiple recollections and anticipations.

Our harvest scene is a moment of the past made present through the writer's art, a process indicated even in the sequence of verb tenses. The novel began in the past but by the third paragraph switched into the historic present; in the passage we have been considering, the historic present remains the governing tense, but for a good part of the paragraph, verbs are omitted entirely, giving way to a series of nouns with participial or adjectival modifiers ("excited faces scrutinizing," "commands, the older men knowing, sternly cautious"), to produce the illusion of an absolute dramatic presence of past objects. All this past, however, is refracted through the consciousness of a particular rememberer, whether we construe him as Daniel Martin or "his ill-concealed ghost" and creator, John Fowles. In fact, from the second paragraph of the novel, where we are told that "The sky's proleptic name was California," we are given small clues that this whole harvest world is seen, as it were, through a telescope, from the distant perspective of some as yet unspecified future. An hour later, after the rabbit hunt, and at the end of the chapter, Daniel Martin will sit alone looking out at the field "Without past or future, purged of tenses; collecting this day, pregnant with being," as an "inscrutable innocent, already in exile" (p. 11). The purging of tenses is precisely what the narrator has just achieved stylistically in evoking the pure presence of the moment; but more generally, language, with its various temporal indicators and mnemonic resources, will allow the narrator (Daniel Martin?) to shuttle between times, to rediscover the past from later perspectives, to feel the subtle and shifting pressures of different pasts on present consciousness—in sum, to follow the precarious moral drift of a life awash in time.

But from what is it that Daniel Martin is "already in exile"? Evidently, from his own past, which is imagined here vanishing away from him even as the aftertaste of its intensity lingers with him. He "collects" the day; soon he will have to recollect it; in midlife, he will be impelled to realize through consciousness and action what the novelist accomplishes in his art, to recuperate the past. The image of the tiny rabbit, darting out momentarily into the observer's field of vision, then disappearing, is not a symbol but an apt dynamic analogy for the teasingly elusive objects of memory and mimesis which the novelistic imagination seeks to fix. "If I had a preferred line in the modern novel," Daniel Martin will note halfway through his story (p. 276), "it was the one that began with Henry James and descended through Virginia Woolf to Nabokov; all, in their different guises, of the confraternity, the secret society, who have known, and known exile from, *la bonne vaux*."

If such novelistic perception of any given present is colored by a sense of the distance traversed from *la bonne vaux*, the "goodly valley" of some remembered early world, the task of the mature imagination is to recollect in fullness without simplifying or sentimentalizing that place in the past from which the self feels itself exiled. That is the essential perspective-setting function of "The Harvest." It is an idyll, a "green pleasance" in Dan's early life in which no roseate aura of nostalgia is allowed to soften the contours and textures of experience, and in which the facts are not forced to mean anything beyond their own ample presence "pregnant with being." It is an idyll with black-and-liver lurchers, swollen-ankled mothers, mangled rabbits, rough-speaking peasants, sun-blistered farm implements. If a criticism directed toward the technical maneuvers of fiction can speak of an "effect of the real," a criticism that seeks to encompass the mimetic objects of fiction might speak also of a "recovery of the real" as both the formal aim and the ultimate point of moral reference for novels like this one.

Daniel Martin in his late forties, perched on a Bel-Air hillside, a smog-smudged panorama of mock-villas and choked freeways spreading out below him, has put himself in a place—geographically, professionally, emotionally—where some vital sense of the real within him is threatened, diminished, confused. It is no wonder that, contemplating a billboard with a giant drum-majorette revolving on top, he is moved to tell his young mistress, a newcomer to this Californian world, "You have to decide one thing here—which is real, you or Los Angeles" (p. 35). Were this a more schematically affirmative novel, the author might have sent his protagonist straight back from this Pacific abode of ontological wooziness to the solid earth of *la bonne vaux* in Devon, but Fowles is keenly aware that time's decree of exile cannot be revoked. "All return is a form of bathos" (p. 203), Daniel Martin shrewdly remarks upon his arrival back in Oxford, when after so many years he is once more in the presence of Jane Mallory. The formal and thematic problem of the novel from this point on is to avoid the bathos and the unrealistic contrivance of a return to the past and yet somehow make Dan nevertheless double back to his point of origin, which is the only vantage-point from which he can see where he really is in the present.

Technically, the novel-form now becomes inevitable for him, or for whoever it is that is writing his story, because it offers the possibility of "a medium that would [be] . . . something dense, interweaving, treating time as horizontal, like a skyline; not cramped, linear and progressive" (p. 331) like the films Dan has been condemned to write. Thematically, it is Jane Mallory who becomes the absorbing object of the would-be novelist's dense, interweaving attention. The way she seems to him, standing simultaneously in two or several widely disparate moments of time, is a constant allurement and a provocation. She is worn down by years of a marriage gone dead, her early beauty abraded by time's passage, a distant stranger now to Daniel Martin; and yet he can see in her, or imagine he sees in her, the intimate friend of a quarter-century past, the fleeting capricious lover of one dreamlike afternoon. Progressively, he comes to perceive Jane as one of those people one very occasionally encounters who uncannily "are catalytic, inherently and unconsciously dissolvent of time and all the naturalist tries to put between himself and his total reality" (p. 413). Getting "whole sight" of Jane is thus obscurely but profoundly entangled with getting whole sight of himself, and that, rather than any romantic or sexual attraction, is why he stubbornly attaches himself to her after her husband's suicide and then drags her with him all the way up the Nile.

The setting, one might be inclined to object, runs the danger of being too patly symbolic, but Fowles manages this personal journey into fabulous antiquity with enough discretion so that it provides resonance for what is gradually happening inside Dan and Jane without seeming like warmed-over D. H. Lawrence. The narrator does observe at a couple of strategic junctures that sailing up that river, the life of its banks virtually as it was in the ancient world, is like a journey not only into Africa but into the heart of time. These occasional passages, however, make their thematic point without melodramatic insistence, and in the foreground of the narrative remain the convincing unromantic figures of Dan and Jane, growing at ease with the warmth of their rediscovered friendship, perplexed by the ambiguities of the bond between them, both of them sensing some hidden wall of alienation which he cannot quite locate and determine how to breach, and which she apparently wants to leave standing.

Daniel Martin's fumbling search for a Jane *perdue* is in fact a signal instance of what I have called Fowles's role as an exemplary novelist. For the primary object of representation and hence of knowledge in the novel as a genre is not scene or event or some image of the historical moment but character, and what Dan's quest for Jane gives us is a patiently realized demonstration of the process of knowing character. I say knowing rather than creating because for Fowles the evident artifice of the novel is there to serve the end of mimesis, of recovering with deepened insight, as art can do, what we experience as moral agents outside the fictional world. Daniel Martin, in other words, is a fictional character and a would-be novelist to boot, but the long effort he needs to make in order to see who Jane is resembles in all but its novelistically granted condition of articulateness what most reasonably reflective people have to undergo in trying honestly to know someone else. Jane has her odd contradictions, but she is finally presented as a characteristic rather than a special case, for it is the generic aptitude of the novel as a slowly unfolding prose narrative medium with fluid access to the consciousness of the personages to be able to render individual identity in its peculiar density and opacity, its shifting combinations of revelation and concealment, fixity and instability. As we all are obliged to perceive each other, Dan can only see Jane from where he stands, and from where he remembers that he stood before. He is afraid he may be glimpsing in her a fantasy of his own invention, and he senses within her a series of dimly apprehended points whose connection he cannot make out. Among the various selves she seems to present is an elusive wraith of the lovely young girl at Oxford; that self, he wants to persuade himself, must also still be alive just as he feels within himself, beneath the archeological layers of later identities, the still potent presence of who he was at twenty-three. The human need for recurrence is reflected almost universally in the artifices of recurrence of narrative literature; but, Dan wonders, might not recurrence also be an inherent structural feature of real events, so that Jane's renewed presence in his life might promise a marriage of the imagined and the real?

Yet perhaps this is a delusion, the bending of a real woman to a mere hypothesis. "I must start treating this woman as she really is," he firmly resolves (p. 483) after he catches himself responding to her with an old reflex of making all the women in his life conform to a single pattern. It is the great virtue of the novel's sober happy ending that a credible way is found for Dan to fulfill this difficult resolution.

After their stay in Egypt, the couple decide, out of an obscure impulse of curiosity, to fly on to Beirut from where they can take a car to see the Krak des Chevaliers, the Crusader castle at Palmyra in Syria. Although the Crusader ruins are of course three millennia more recent than the Egyptian antiquities they have been viewing, as the fortress actually appears in the novel, isolated and abandoned in a wintry landscape swathed in bone-chilling fog, it has the effect of a remote past deeply recessed within all the other pasts they have experienced. Confronted by the labyrinthine plan and the "stupefying unnecessity" of this once elegant structure in the middle of nowhere, and now without the interfering presence of other tourists, Dan and Jane feel driven in upon each other. The last act of the hesitant shadow-play they have been conducting with each other is then precipitated by external circumstance. In the primitive little inn at the foot of the Krak des Chevaliers where they are to spend the night, Jane is forced to abandon her room because the fumes of the paraffin stove are asphyxiating and it is too cold to sleep without heat. In a gesture of wry resignation, she concludes that she is too old to make a fuss about such matters, and so she accepts Dan's invitation to sleep in his room, in his bed. Thus, in this strange and forbidding setting, between rough, clammy sheets, they renew the physical intimacy they shared just once, two and a half decades before.

Or so it might seem. The novelist's perception of this culminating moment is in fact too complex for him to subscribe without qualification either to the renewal or to the intimacy. Real relationships, he suggests, are much harder than that. Fowles's rendering of the long-postponed act of love is worth looking at, for it strikingly illustrates how mimesis in the novel is directed toward a stubbornly disorderly class of perceptual, relational, and attitudinal human realities not readily accessible to other media of representation.

> It seemed to him, as they let sexual feeling dominate the next few minutes, that someone else was aroused, had taken over her body. It was not that she remained passive; the arms did rise and the hands caressed in return; but that in some paradoxical way made it seem a ritual, a concession

to physical convention. For once in his life he would have liked his partner to talk, to know what she felt. He had pushed back the bedclothes and his own eyes, now accustomed to the dark, kept searching her face for answers; and even when they were joined, failed to get them. Her body excited him more than he expected—in the dim light from the fire it still looked, was young: slender-armed, small-breasted . . . and that side of it came almost as a last secret she had kept, an added unfairness.

Yet it did not take place as he had dreamed, did not reach that non-physical climax he wanted, fused melting of all further doubt. She had been wiser in not expecting it; though he still felt obscurely cheated by her not trying to create what she had not expected. But nor, finally, was she merely indulging him, comforting him. For a brief while she was the female animal; possessive, wanting possession to endure. It came to him, immediately afterward, when he was still lying half across her, that the failure could have been put in terms of grammatical person. It had happened in the third, when he craved the first and second.

It left, too, a sad, sour little presentiment of age, of the death of the illusion that they could find each other as simply as this. It was too small, too short, too childlike a thing. (p. 599).

By this late point in the novel, Fowles has set aside his polemic invocations of cinema, but the terms he chooses for representing this sexual act are extravagantly uncinematic, or to put it positively, quintessentially novelistic. Heterosexual coitus necessarily involves the physical joining of male animal and female animal, and some contemporary American novelists in their *de rigeur* rutting scenes try to write as if this were all that was involved; in any case, film with its visual immediacy is much better at rendering that side of things. An opposite view of sexual union takes it as a mystical or metaphysical occasion, something Dan comes close to in his hope of finding a "non-physical climax" in which he will quite literally embrace the past. The transcendent aspect of the erotic, of course, has been treated by certain lyric novelists like Lawrence and has been variously if clumsily attempted in contemporary cinema with soft-focus images of naked bodies moving with balletic grace to a richly melodic soundtrack. What I would take to be the more characteristic province of the novel in the representation of the erotic is the large middle ground between these two extremes. Daniel Martin takes cognizance of both animal fact and metaphysical aspiration, but his imagination of this sexual moment is the perception of one separate person trying to fathom another across the chasm of different pasts, different fears and fantasies, different moral characters.

The dense, interweaving attention he brings to bear on the experience can comprehend within one verbal structure of paradox not only the ambiguous entanglement of present and past but of mind and body, of one side of the psyche and another.

The novelist exploits here two general expressive possibilities of his verbal medium: the ability to follow the serial movement of a mind thinking through words, and the ability intelligibly to state internal divisions or oppositions, conditions contrary to each other or to seeming fact. Jane in the act of passion, then, is both herself and someone else; her physical responsiveness is, in the ratiocinative language through which her lover tries to understand it, not the spontaneous motions of erotic pleasuring but a ritual, a concession to convention. The passage as a whole, using a strategy that has been explored by certain maturely knowing novelists beginning with the Stendhal of *Lucien Leuwen*, defines the experience in question through a series of statements about what it is not, or about what the character would have liked it to be. (The conditional and the subjunctive, I would suggest, are the novelistic verbal modes *par excellence*.) The passage bristles with nots and nors, reinforced by logical transition-words like but and yet. It is perfectly appropriate that Dan should make the post-climactic discovery that grammar itself provides the aptest terms for describing what he was looking for and failed to find. In this age after Structuralism Fowles, however old-fashioned it may seem to some, remains true to a dominant generic assumption of the novel in his confidence that language with its formal properties can give us at least some of the handles we need to grasp the realities of psychology and relation.

The whole process, moreover, of getting complexities right by getting them into language is formulated as a summary of the protagonist's reactions which incorporates certain distinct elements of narrated monologue, the technique of presentation that reenacts in third person the mental kinesis of the character in the midst of his experience. When, for example, Dan finds himself surprisingly aroused by Jane's nakedness, the interior rhythm of perception, reflection, and reversal is caught in the syntax and the sequence of the words: "Her body excited him more than he expected—in the dim light from the fire it still looked, was young: slender-armed, small breasted . . . and that side of it came almost as a last secret she had kept, an added unfairness." The appropriately uncertain firelight in which he sees her body of course facilitates his perception of it as still a young woman's body; the self-correction of "looked, was young" mimes the mental process by which the character insists on the identity between appearance and reality, on the literal presence of the past. Then, after the three suspension points inserted by the novelist, the protagonist "places" this new revelation of Jane against everything that has happened between him and her in the preceding weeks, but the final appositional phrase, "an added unfairness," at once takes us a little by surprise and immediately convinces us by its psychological rightness: it is not a sense of delight but an edge of resentment that Dan feels in the discovery of this unexpectedly youthful body, for it is a culminating instance of how Jane has withheld herself from him when he offered candid intimacy. This mode of presentation, then, conveys a persuasive sense of how complicated each of us is with others and with himself not by a psychological analysis of motives but, as novelists associating the narrative point of view with that of their protagonists have often done so well, by reproducing the minute and sometimes unforeseen fluctuations of the mind weighing its relations with others and with itself.

The next, and decisive, dialectic swing in Dan's pursuit of a lost Jane is that the failure and the exposure of illusion are followed by a quiet intimation that the quest may in fact be close to realization. Holding her in the dark as their bodies wait for sleep, he begins to feel that somehow now they at last know each other, "that this innocent, silent nakedness was a nearer, deeper thing than the love-making; that they were more coupled, thus" (pp. 600–01). The two remaining chapters of dénouement flow directly from this moment of fulfillment. After another day of oscillation and doubt, Jane resolves to live with Dan; he sees now that he must really put Hollywood behind him, resume his Englishness, and in joining with this woman who is part of his past, he must also turn to the novel, as the art-form that can densely interweave the multiple truths of living through consciousness in more than one time. Amidst these resolutions of renewal, life persists in its untidiness: Dan can move beyond the preceding phase of his emotional history only after going through a pained last meeting in London with his actress friend, and at the very end, before returning to Jane and domestic warmth, he is led to wonder whether he may be deluding himself about his capacity for putting his life into verbal art as a novel.

This final surge of doubt is aptly triggered by an art-work, the late Rembrandt self-portrait in the manor on Hampstead Heath into whose presence Dan wanders. The canvas shows him "a presentness beyond all time and language; a puffed face, a pair of rheumy eyes, and a profound and unassuageable vision." That unflinching, strangely aloof countenance seems to judge Daniel Martin, to strike him with consternation, in its having "said all he had never managed to say and would never manage to say." (The novel he wants to write is of course also a self-portrait.) And yet the timeless image Rembrandt made of himself stares from the canvas "out of the entire knowledge of his own genius and of the inadequacy of genius before human reality" (p. 628). The Rembrandt self-portrait, that is, both humbles the would-be novelist and strengthens his resolve, for if it demonstrates a mastery that dwarfs the efforts of any ordinary artist, it also conveys to him an awareness that mimesis is, for all representational artists including the greatest, never a consummation but an exacting task to be undertaken, and undertaken again. Art is deep but human reality remains in part resistant to it, exposing many vivid facets to the light of representation, keeping others, perhaps some of the most essential, hidden in a penumbra of ambiguity, enigma, doubt. This double awareness has often been richly suggested by the novel through its capaciousness, its narrative and meditative amplitude as an instrument of mimesis. That in the end is what *Daniel Martin* succeeds in doing, in being: it is at once a rather traditional novel and an acutely self-conscious one that bears witness to the undiminished vitality of the genre.

NOTES

1. John Fowles, *Daniel Martin* (Boston: Little, Brown and Company, 1977), p. 8. All subsequent references are to this edition.

Notes on the Novel-as-Autobiography

Peter Bailey
St. Lawrence University

We are used enough by now to hearing works such as Benjamin Franklin's *Memoirs* and Vladimir Nabokov's *Speak, Memory* discussed as forms of literary fiction[1] that the obverse concept—the novel-as-autobiography, or the novel, in Tony Tanner's phrase, of "fictionalized recall"[2]—may not seem a particularly anomalous one either. Perhaps it should—or perhaps we should at least consider the anomaly such a form would have represented to a period in which generic labels seemed more helpful, and less fluid and ambiguous, than they do to us. It was toward the close of such a period, significantly, that Wayne Booth in *The Rhetoric of Fiction* rehearsed the critical controversy surrounding *A Portrait of the Artist as a Young Man*, attributing the existence of discordant and apparently irreconcilable interpretations of the novel to a clash implicit in it between Joyce's autobiographical materials and the genre—literary realism—in which he was working. Booth found it understandable that some critics considered the novel so inextricably bound up with Joyce's own boyhood experiences as to imply an authorial endorsement of and sympathy for Stephen, while others believed the autobiographical elements to have been ironized and absorbed completely into the novel's aesthetic plan, and he blamed the confusion partially upon Joyce's complexly ambivalent attitude toward his youthful self-projection. Equally contributory to the rhetorical irresolution of *Portrait*, Booth contended, was the absence of conventions and precedents within the realistic tradition which might have guided Joyce in the successful translation of autobiography into art, and thus he argued that, however great the novel is conceded to be, there comes a point at which it obliges us to seek clarifications in the life of the author rather than in that of the character, and to that extent its effectiveness is compromised.[3]

We are somewhat more tolerant, these days, of novels which deliberately conduct us back toward the gratuitous complexities of existence rather than toward artfully contrived, all-encompassing aesthetic resolutions than was Booth, and we probably appreciate the life-art intricacies in which A *Portrait* necessarily embroils us more than he did as well. But the lesson of the extent to which Joyce was able to turn his specific personal experience into art has not been lost on us either, and it is no exaggeration to suggest that the new autobiographical fiction being pioneered in recent years owes its inspiration and facilitating conception to Joyce's success in shaping the ragged stuff of autobiography into aesthetic form. Implicit in Joyce's *Portrait* achievement, this is to say, is the idea that the self can be fictionalized, metaphorized, molded into more or less objective aesthetic configurations if imagination and craft enough are applied to the task. It is but a short step, then, from this idea to the recognition that any presentation of the self through language is necessarily a selection, a fragment, a fiction, and it is this recognition which, for instance, allows Jorge Luis Borges to appear in his own fictions as narrator/character, and this recognition too which permits writers such as Ronald Sukenick, Frank Conroy and Frederick Exley to write novels about characters who bear their own names and who are deliberately simplified, artfully crafted projections of themselves. Thus, the novel-as-autobiography.

Inserting a fictionalized projection of the self into a novel is the easy part of the autobiographical novelist's task, however; the more difficult job is the same as it is in the composition of any novel, autobiographical or not—that of manipulating the chosen materials toward the establishment of a structural tension which will sustain the breadth of the work and supply it with a discernible beginning, middle, and end. Since it is a primary aim of Sukenick's work to repudiate many of the artifices of fiction which isolate it from the contingencies of experienced life, his introduction of himself (and of a few literary friends as well) into his novels is undertaken in the spirit of deliberate generic apostasy.[4] Conroy and Exley, on the other hand, want both novelistic completion and a sense of gratuitous life in their books, both formal resolution and the sense of casual, incidental, open-ended experience as well. They are confronting in their novels, then, precisely the problem that Booth saw Joyce struggling with in *Portrait*, and it is in this very struggle between autobiography and art, between literary form and life, that they find the structural tension which transforms Conroy's "autobiographical narrative" and Exley's "fictional memoir" into fully accomplished, completely achieved novels.

To see how autobiographical material can be manipulated so as to facilitate (rather than, as we have habitually thought, to impede) the achievement of an aesthetic resolution in a work of fiction, it will be useful to compare the structural coherence of the novel-as-autobiography to the aesthetic cohesion engendered in the more conventional and familiar autobiographical novel. In this latter novel the autobiographical materials are translated into aesthetic ones through an act of creative imagination, details from life altered and rearranged by the author in order that his art—not his life—be allowed to dictate the various contiguities, convergences and ironies which appear in his book. However much we are aware, for example, that Peter Caldwell, the *bildungsroman* protagonist and principal narrator of *The Centaur*, significantly resembles John Updike when he was a teenager,[5] we respond to him appropriately enough as a fictional character, recognizing the necessity of his fictionality to the aesthetic scheme of Updike's novel and seeing in his dissimilarities to his creator signs of the presence of a deliberate artistic plan. We understand, too, that Peter's situation (he is a "failed expressionist painter" living with a mistress in the Bohemian inelegance of a Manhattan loft) at the time of his nostalgic recounting of his embarrassed, exasperating, adolescent love for his father comments eloquently on the very events he is relating, the sacrifices his father made on his behalf and the unceasing misery he encountered in his attempts to restore his family to lower middle class solvency juxtaposed evocatively against the coolly cosmopolitan, decadent world into which Peter has retreated. Peter's narration, then, is an attempt to communicate across the gulf which now separates his present life from the life he lived in his father's home, the disparity between these two discontinuous worlds effectively dramatizing one of the novel's central concerns—Peter's question, "Was it for this that my father gave up his life?"[6]

Even as we recognize the purpose and effectiveness of Updike's reinvention and ironization of the autobiographical elements of *The Centaur*, we must understand too the price this thorough dissevering of the novel from its experiential roots entails. It is clear enough that Peter's narration reflects his attempt to celebrate, and to an extent to redeem, the sacrifices his father made for his sake, and thus that the narration itself represents his attempt to answer in the affirmative the very question which is so central to it. This is the point at which form and content successfully merge in this section of the novel, of course, Peter's narration achieving self-referentiality through the fact that its existence answers the question that it poses. The satisfactory resolution of the son's relationship to his father on this level, however, invites—perhaps even demands—an extra-textual speculation that the novel's existence represents a similar sort of resolution on the autobiographical plane, that it is Updike's way of doing for his father what Peter in his narrative sections does for his. The patently autobiographical nature of *The Centaur* necessarily prompts such conjectures, but it supplies us with no means of confirming or repudiating them, largely because, unlike Peter's narrative, the existence of Updike's narrative bears little relation to the contents of it. In other words, the fact that *The Centaur* exists as a book bears only an indeterminate relation to the issues the book itself raises, and thus the novel assumes a strictly conventional (as opposed to thematically significant) relationship between itself and the world; *The Centaur* is a self-enclosed, self-perpetuating literary world whose connection to the world around it is traditional (it says on the cover that it is a novel, and we treat it as we treat objects in that class) and vague (the relationship between its author and its primary narrator is obvious but ambiguous). Like most autobiographical novels of this kind, *The Centaur* affirms, through its own self-referentiality, a necessary and unbreachable gap between the inner worlds of novels and the external world in which they sit on bookshelves (the very disparity, of course, which Sukenick's work strives to eliminate), and thus it leaves us with a residual, confused awareness that the autobiographical underpinnings of the novel are at once insistently present and at the same time to be dismissed as extraneous and irrelevant to the real issues of the work. Rather than regarding this penumbral ambiguity of autobiographical fiction as a problem, Updike sees it as a necessary by-product of the artistic exchange involved in translating life into art.[7]

Although the elimination of this ambiguity may not be a primary purpose of the novel-as-autobiography developed by Conroy and Exley, its elimination is one of the effects of their presenting projections of themselves as characters in their novels. The explanation for this is simply that the existence of their books comments upon and generates a structural closure of the narratives contained in their novels' pages. Conroy's *Stop-time* accomplishes this movement more straightforwardly and less complexly than does *A Fan's Notes*, and thus we will use it to clarify the mechanics of the novel-as-autobiography before proceeding to consider its workings in more detail in Exley's novel.

What transforms *Stop-time* from a conventional autobiographical novel into a novel-as-autobiography is Conroy's use of a fictionalized projection of himself as his protagonist, the effect of which is to establish a necessary tension between the conflict that the character is trying to resolve and the book itself, between the author Conroy and the protagonist Conroy. The conflict that protagonist Conroy (henceforth Frank) is attempting to resolve consists in his contradictory impulses toward the extinction of consciousness (which he approaches in nightly speeding binges in his Jaguar, his mind becoming "suddenly clean and white, washed out by the danger and the wind") and the subjugation of his experience to the organizing, conceptualizing capacities of consciousness (at eleven he had waited for some "momentous event" to happen which would "clear away the trivia and throw my life into proper perspective"[8]). These impulses are, in an important respect, the same impulse: they both imply the stopping of time's passage, and they are both symptomatic as well of Frank's inability to come to terms with his past. "My acceptance at a good college," he explains in the last chapter of the book, "meant I could destroy my past. It seemed to me to amount to an order to destroy my past, a past I didn't understand, a past I feared and a past with which I expected to be forever encumbered" (p. 295).

One can destroy his past by extinguishing the consciousness in which it is preserved (thus Frank's recurrent flirtations with suicide), but it is obvious that Frank is finally more concerned with coming to terms with his past than with annihilating it, and in early adolescence he discovers what will ultimately become the medium of that coming to terms: books. "I could not resist the clarity of the world of books," he explains, "the incredibly satisfying way in which life became weighty and accessible. Books were reality. I hadn't made up my mind about my own life, a vague, dreamy affair, amorphous and dimly perceived, without beginning or end" (p. 149). *Stop-time*, clearly enough, shapes that amorphousness and organizes its beginning and endlessness into coherent sequence,[9] but beyond this, the book's existence itself represents Conroy's attainment of a self-possession, purposefulness and acceptance (or at least circumscription) of the past which Frank never fully achieves. Conroy does, however, close his book with a symbolic merging of himself with his protagonist, the novel's epilogue allowing the latter to experience on the narrative plane an approximation of what Conroy experiences in having completed the novel: stop-time.

The epilogue narrates the culmination of one of Frank's wild drives in a collision with a fountain, the exhilarating sense of imminent death giving way suddenly to the restoration of normalcy. "But the front wheel caught a low curb and the car spun around the fountain like a baton around a cheerleader's wrist. I became disoriented, knowing only that something freakish was happening. The side of the car bumped very gently against the fountain, inches away from my face. Then, with a slight lurch, everything stopped" (p. 304). This moment is only a pale echo of the fixing of motion which the novel accomplishes, but this is at once appropriate and unavoidable, since the novel has to be written for that more all-encompassing stop-time to be effected. Frank can never know the completed motion, in other words, because he is only an agent of that completed movement's achievement. The problem that Frank is on the road to solving in *Stop-time* is the very problem to which, for Conroy, *Stop-time* is the solution.

The completion of the novel allows Conroy too to come as close as he ever will to achieving the state he describes earlier in the novel, a state which nicely articulates the basic paradox which lies at the heart of the novel-as-autobiography. Frank recalls accidentally running into a car as a boy, remembering that the collision made him feel like a funny papers figure with stars and planets revolving giddily about his head. "It seemed I was a comic strip character," he explains, "a cartoon somehow living out the plot and reading it simultaneously" (p. 37).

What Frank Conroy finds in the world of books, Frederick Exley finds in the world of professional football. Sitting in a bar in Watertown, New York, awaiting the kickoff of a televised game between his beloved New York Giants and the Dallas Cowboys, Exley recalls the fascination the sport has always held for him. "Why did football bring me so to life?" he asks himself.

> Part of it was my feeling that football was an island of directness in a world of circumspection. In football a man was asked to do a difficult and often brutal job, and he either did it or got out. There was nothing rhetorical or vague about it; I chose to believe it was not unlike the jobs all men, in some sunnier past, had been called upon to do. It smacked of something old, something traditional, something unclouded by legerdemain and subterfuge. It had that kind of power over me, drawing me back with the force of

something known, something remembered, as elusive as integrity—perhaps it was nothing more than the force of forgotten childhood. Whatever it was, I gave myself up to the Giants utterly. The recompense I gained was the feeling of being alive.[10]

Unable to imagine an existence for himself as vivid, significant or satisfying as a Sunday afternoon football game, Exley passes each week throughout the autumn and into winter in a state of morose indolence, living on only in anticipation of the pregame "nervous light of Sunday" when his life will begin once again to gain sustenance from and be lent a second-hand intelligibility by the game's reflected sense of purpose and coherence. Where Exley's world is vague, haphazard and only provisionally real, football's is exact, explicit and direct, these qualities demonstrated in every play as thoroughly as Exley's are exemplified in his every moment of indecision and inaction. The directness and finality of a run by Frank Gifford (Exley's primary hero) or a Chuck Bednarik tackle are important to Exley not only for what they accomplish, but for what they protect from as well. He values the purposefulness and certainty of the world of football and responds so fanatically to it because he knows all too well what directionless means and what it can drive its victim to. "Suicide," he writes, "is the most eloquent of all wails for direction. Suicide is what Hemingway does when the world gets so out of focus that he can no longer commit it to paper. Suicide is what the man does when the pain caused by the cancer of the bowel blurs the landscape to the eye so that all things look the same and even the defined direction of darkness seems welcome" (p. 136). Exley, the epitome of the directionless man, does not commit suicide, of course; he instead commits the world to paper in the "eloquent wail" which is the novel, A Fan's Notes.

But just as Stop-time obliges us ultimately to distinguish between Conroy the author and Frank the character, so A Fan's Notes requires that a similar distinction be drawn between Exley the author and Frederick the character, a distinction that much more difficult to draw because Frederick seems, throughout the course of the narrative, to be writing—or at least trying to write—the very book we are reading. This added element of the composition of the novel being a central concern of the character in it accounts for the greater technical and structural complexity of A Fan's Notes, and also explains why a novel so carefully crafted and meticulously ironized was so often criticized for being autobiographically self-indulgent.[11] Whereas Stop-time generates one stable ironic tension between its own existence and the life that the character in it is trying to make sense of, *A Fan's Notes* establishes a dynamic irony between Frederick's futile attempts to write a novel and Exley's ability to use those very materials toward the creation of the novel his protagonist is unable to compose.

In an introductory note to the reader, Exley the author (hereafter Exley) explains that his book is only loosely patterned on the real events of his own life, and that much of it is purely fictional. "I have drawn freely from the imagination," his note concludes. "To this extent and for this reason I ask to be judged as a writer of fantasy." (This brief explanatory note, a sort of poor man's "Custom-House" chapter, echoes Hawthorne's comment in his preface to *The Scarlet Letter*: " . . . we may prate of the circumstances that lie around us, and even of ourself, but still keep the inmost Me behind the veil. To this extent and within these limits an author, methinks, may be autobiographical, without violating either the reader's rights or his own."[12]) His admonition delivered, Exley withdraws, and although the unwary reader might assume that he returns on page one to narrate the book, it is in fact Frederick who takes over at that point. Frederick is responsible for the writing of the notes of a fan which make up the book since he, by his own admission, is incapable of writing a novel. It is Exley, then, who writes the completed and self-enclosed novel, *A Fan's Notes*, the novel Frederick can never know is present-in-potential within his notes.

Frederick's dilemma (which, like Frank's, is resolved by the existence of the novel in which it is presented) is a complexly circular one which revolves around his desire for fame, the drinking and fantasy in which he indulges himself as a consolation for his famelessness, and the mental instability which is the consequence of these responses. Early in his narration, Frederick explains that his primary goal in life had been to achieve fame, a dream which is, as the novel's epigraph from Hawthorne suggests, "more powerful than a thousand realities." Remembering the fame that his father had won for his athletic exploits at Watertown High School and with the local Red & Black semi-professional football team, Frederick sees fame as his birthright, as an heirloom which should rightfully have fallen to him upon the death of his father. This apparently simple dream of fame is complicated by the fact that Frederick has nothing but contempt for those people—the American populace—who confer fame upon those they deem worthy of it. (Thus the novel's second epigraph, from Dylan Thomas, "All Wales is like this. I have a friend who writes long and entirely unprintable verses beginning, 'What are you, Wales, but a tired old bitch?' and 'Wales my country, Wales my sow.' ") Frederick, consequently, finds himself in the impossible position of wanting something the achievement of which can only result in the loss of his self-respect. Complementing this conflict, is another, equally circular, one. Aware that his ambivalence toward fame has incapacitated him, has left him impotently yearning for a state which he knows better than to want, he finds that, by his own definition, as well as by the definition of the society responsible for imposing the conflict upon him, his inability to act is a form of insanity. While part of him recognizes the justice of the society's ascription of insanity to him,[13] then, his emotions object that to conform to a society which is by its own definition insane is to submit to that insanity at the cost of a repudiation of his own feelings about what human sanity really is. Thus does Frederick, ensnared in a pure state of Catch-22, retreat to his mother's davenport in Watertown, there to patiently await the "nervous light of Sunday" and the temporary resurrection of a linear, coherent world.

While confined to that davenport Frederick passes his time in fantasizing, but he is careful to insist that the fantasizing was not the cause of his insanity—it was, instead, one of its necessary results: "I was never incapacitated by fantasy," he writes, "I had incapacitated myself; the fantasy had followed to consume the endlessly idle hours" (p. 80). His fantasies were not even particularly original ones, he admits, and contained much of the vulgarly megalomaniac dross discernible in the dreams of many of his fellow average Americans. In one of them he owns the New York Giants, has women swooning at his feet and dines only in restaurants born of some "Playboy After Hours" column; in another he is a British colonist in Rhodesia, charming the natives into sparing his life as they brutally do in his imperialist colleagues; in a third he turns a TV soap opera into a pornographic romp replete with all the latest perversions, the production employing all the newest erotic camera techniques. Having regaled the reader with these fantasies, Frederick is quick to point out that he has never mistaken them for realities, that he knows the difference between fact and fantasy. Referring to his Giants' ownership fantasy, he writes, "I never for a second lived this fantasy. There was always one 'I,' aloof and ironical, watching the other me play out 'his' tawdry dreams" (p. 80). A gratuitous enough apologia on Frederick's part, these lines represent, from

Exley's perspective, one of the few explicit references in the novel to the game he has set up between himself as author and his fictionalized self-projection. The "aloof and ironical" one, clearly enough, is Exley; the "other me" is Frederick, a character living out "tawdry dreams" and painfully recording them as well, thoroughly innocent of the knowledge that the experiences he is so self-laceratingly recalling are fictions devised by his fabricator, "creations solely of the imagination" as Exley has it in the novel's prefatory note.[14] The novel's title might well be amended to read *A Fan(tasy)'s Notes* once this two-dimensional narrative mechanics is recognized, and in its light many lines which had previously seemed mere declarative statements come to be seen as further clues to the existence of Exley above and beyond Frederick's disorderly attempt at writing a novel.

Having decided that his only hope for fame lies in writing, Frederick imagines himself producing the "Big Book" and imposing himself "deep into the mentality of his countrymen" (p. 99). He struggles with the book for a time, but must finally recognize that his effort has been wasted, that he lacks the technical skills to write a successful novel and that his dreams of fame must come to nothing in light of this realization. Seeing the final dishonesty of his lifelong identification with Frank Gifford (whom he had met briefly while both were undergraduates at U.S.C.), he confesses finally that "where I could not, with syntax, give shape to my fantasies, Gifford could, with his superb timing, his great hands, his uncanny faking, give shape to his" (p. 134), and it is not long before these truths give way to a final, shattering Truth. Remembering a brawl he had precipitated in Greenwich Village on the night following the game in which Gifford's career was ended by an injury, Frederick recalls that "I fought because I understood, and could not bear to understand, that it was my destiny—unlike that of my father, whose fate it was to hear the roar of the crowd—to sit in the stands with most men and acclaim others. It was my fate, my destiny, my end, to be a fan" (p. 357).

Although Frederick remains nothing more than a fan at the end of the novel, an anonymous man besieged in his own fantasy by Americans as faceless as himself, his creation has exalted his creator out of the realm of fandom and has allowed him to become, as Roger Sale noticed, a writer who has fans.[15] The difference between their two fates, of course, lies in the difference between the books they have written.

One of the books presented in the volume titled *A Fan's Notes* is a book of notes compiled by a fan, a demonstration of Frederick's inability to create a consistent, coherent novel. His book is loose, improvised, the work of a man whose sorrows are too deep and his humiliations too great to allow him to objectify and transform them into the stuff of art. Although there are occasional dramatic climaxes and thematic convergences in his book, they are incidental ones, never coalescing into anything approaching a deliberate and all-pervading aesthetic plan.

Exley's counter-book (we are reminded, perhaps, of the Tlönian standard of Jorge Luis Borges, which dictates that "a book that does not contain its counter-book is considered incomplete"[16]) is of a totally different sort. Tightly structured and tense with motifs, thematic patterns and artistic unities, Exley's novel serves as a perfect counterpoint to Frederick's strictly autobiographical notes, the gratuitous anecdotes in the latter transformed into significant revelations in the former, incidental details in Frederick's narrative representing thematic culminations in Exley's, and so on.

To cite two examples of the disparity which exists between Frederick's understanding of his narrative and Exley's view of it, we notice first that Frederick encounters three figures in the novel who seem even to him to be somewhat larger than life, and who, coincidentally, all have names beginning with B. He recognizes that Bunny Sue Allorgee is his ideal—everyone's ideal—of the midwestern American girl, the unsurpassed Big Ten cheerleader of male fantasy; he sees too that Mr. Blue is the very embodiment of the American salesman, a man obsessed with making the ultimate sale and tasting the fruits of it; he understands as well that Bumpy Plumpton, who becomes his brother-in-law, is the American vulgarian nonpareil, a man who delights in trivializing the nation's poetic utterances and whose capacity for self-hatred is outstripped only by his boundless capacity for the consumption of food and drink and things. Frederick comprehends that these are all rather extreme types, then, but he doesn't take in that each of them is an archetype of some American characteristic who Exley has placed in his path in order to test and mock Frederick's own conspicuously American tastes, impulses and desires. These three are all, to alter Bunny Sue's name slightly, allegories, and Frederick's inability to recognize this points up the distance between his memoir and Exley's symbolic narrative. (Frederick's comment on the sports pages applies equally well to the novel in which he appears, then: amid all the clamor it becomes "difficult for the fan to isolate the real from the fantastic" [p. 131].)

The final scene of the novel points up with equal clarity the difference between Frederick's and Exley's *A Fan's Notes*. For Frederick, the recurrent dream he describes in the book's closing pages represents a dramatization of his inability to resolve the conflict which has been his from the beginning. The cashmere-sweatered, Bermuda-shorted heirs of the Great Society toward whom he is obsessively drawn in the dream represent at once the audience he needs, as well as the audience he needs to berate for their divergence from human integrity and decency as he understands them, and thus his simultaneous failures to pass them by indifferently (suggesting the abandonment of this dream of fame) and to confront them without succumbing to a beating at their hands (suggesting his inability to ever engage or convert them) image up the extent to which he remains incapacitated by the tension which exists between his desires and his possibilities, between his ambitions and his actual circumstances. For Exley, on the other hand, this final scene represents Frederick's frustration and desperate impotence raised to the level of epiphany, and constitutes the resonant climax of a fully achieved, deliberately conceived novel. For both Frederick and Exley this recurrent dream enacts an epiphany, then, but for Frederick it is an epiphany of perpetual and terminal defeat, whereas for Exley it is an epiphany whose effectiveness represents the closure of the work which constitutes his own transcendence of Frederick's conflict. [17]

To make so much of the ironic relationship implicit in Exley's narrative is to make his novel sound like a protracted joke at its protagonist's expense; in fact, the novel is extremely serious—almost oppressively so—and uses the notes-within-the-novel structure less as a joke than as a technical device aimed at distancing Exley from his fictional counterpart. It is no doubt safe to assume that a number of Frederick's conflicts were—or are—Exley's as well, and a propensity for fantasy, as central as it is in the novel, is probably one of these. Having had Frederick admit that these fantasies arose out of "some deep inability to live with myself," Exley suggests one purpose he had in mind in writing the book and hints as well why he wants to be judged as a "writer of fantasy." Put simply, he has managed to channel his life-denying fantasies (as Frederick was never able to do) into a realm which could accommodate them without destroying him—the realm of his novel.

Early in *A Fan's Notes* Frederick speaks of his desire to relate his numerous problems to an analyst, and his mocking tone does little to undermine the sense of sincerity behind his admission. "I wanted to explore this [sexual] fantasy with a doctor in the hope that, once uttered, it would . . . be gone forever. I wanted to lie hour after hour on a couch, pouring out the dark secret places of my heart—do this feeling that over my shoulder sat humanity and wisdom and generosity, a munificent heart—do this until that incredibly lovely day when the great man would say to me, his voice grave and dramatic with discovery: 'This is you, Exley. Rise and go out into the world a whole man' " (p. 81). For Frederick no such resolution is possible, for his book ends with the recurrent dream image of himself constantly, obsessively running toward a brutal confrontation. But Exley's novel has, symbolically at least, done for him what the doctor would have: it has allowed him to pour out "the dark secret places of his heart" to an audience, the effect of which has been to make of him "a whole man." We discover this when we realize that his book lasts a page longer than does Frederick's, the "About the Author" paragraph at the end of the volume presenting Exley as the conventional sort of fellow about whom coherent "About the Author" blurbs can be written. Exley has indeed emerged from *A Fan's Notes* "a whole man."[18]

Human psychological conflicts like those addressed in the pages of *Stop-time* and *A Fan's Notes* are neither so simple nor so malleable as to be instantly resolved through their projection into works of fiction, of course, and it would be misleading and irresponsible to make extravagant claims for the psychological efficacy of these novels based solely on the internal evidence of the texts. To "throw one's life into proper perspective," as Conroy seeks to do by projecting it into a novel, may, after all, leave him with nothing more than a life thrown into literary perspective.

There are, nonetheless, two unmistakable and distinctly positive effects of novels-as-autobiography like Conroy's and Exley's: first, they deliberately undermine the traditional and largely spurious authority of the novelist by depriving him of his privileged position above and beyond the work. (He necessarily remains something like Stephen Dedalus' artist-god, but he can no longer be quite so indifferent because of his personal stake in the novel's action.) And second, they narrow the gap which exists between fiction and autobiography, a gap which (as John Fowles' narrator argues in *The French Lieutenant's Woman* in a passage Exley excerpts for an epigraph for *Pages from a Cold Island*) may have been artificial to begin with. "A character is either 'real' or 'imaginary'?" Fowles' narrator asks,

> If you think that, *hypocrite lecteur*, I can only smile. You do not think of your own past as quite real; you dress it up, gild it or blacken it, censor it, tinker with it . . . fictionalize it, in a word, and put it away on a shelf—your book, your romanced autobiography. We are all in flight from real reality. That is the basic definition of Homo Sapiens.[19]

NOTES

1. This argument is advanced by, among others, David Levin, "*The Autobiography of Benjamin Franklin*: The Puritan Experimenter in Life and Art," *Yale Review*, 53 (1964), 258–76; and J. A. Leo LeMay, "Benjamin Franklin in *Major Writers of Early American Literature* (Madison, Wisc.: University of Wisconsin Press, 1972), pp. 238–42.

2. Tony Tanner, *City of Words* (New York: Harper & Row, 1971), pp. 316–21.

3. Wayne Booth, *The Rhetoric of Fiction* (Chicago: University of Chicago Press, 1961), pp. 323–39.

4. Sukenick discusses his reservations concerning the traditional autobiographical novel and the conventions it relies upon in an interview with Joe David Bellamy, citing Conroy's *Stop-time* as "an autobiography influenced by the Victorian novel." See *The New Fiction: Interviews with Innovative American Writers*, ed. Joe David Bellamy (Urbana, Ill.: University of Illinois Press, 1974), p. 57.

5. Updike has admitted the autobiographical basis of *The Centaur*, explaining in an interview that it is his own adolescence he is recasting in that novel and in his other Olinger-based works, and that "George Caldwell was assembled from certain vivid gestures and plights characteristic of [his father] Wesley Updike." "John Updike Interview," in *Writers at Work: The Paris Review Interviews, Fourth Series* (New York: Penguin Books, 1977), p. 270.

6. John Updike, *The Centaur* (New York: Alfred A. Knopf, 1963), p. 270.

7. In his *Paris Review* interview, Updike explains that "I disavow any essential connection between my life and whatever I write. I think it's a morbid and inappropriate concern. . . . But the work, the words on paper, must stand apart from our living presences; we sit down at the desk and become nothing but the excuse for the husks we cast off." *Writers at Work*, pp. 433–34.

8. Frank Conroy, *Stop-time* (New York: Viking Press, 1967), p. 19. All subsequent references are to this edition, and will be noted parenthetically in the text.

9. Roger Ramsey provides a detailed demonstration of the extent to which the facts of *Stop-time* are manipulated and shaped for aesthetic purposes in "The Illusion of Fiction in Frank Conroy's *Stop-time*," *Modern Fiction Studies*, 20 (1974), 391–99.

10. Frederick Exley, *A Fan's Notes* (New York: Harper & Row, 1968), p. 8. All subsequent references are to this edition, and are noted parenthetically in the text.

11. To cite but one such comment, Stanley Reynolds (*New Statesman* [January 30, 1970], p. 158) objects that the effect of *A Fan's Notes* is "rather like getting buttonholed by a drunk in a bar who grips you by both lapels, breathing whiskey and polysyllables in your face. . . . "

12. Nathaniel Hawthorne, *The Scarlet Letter*, ed. Sculley Bradley et al. (New York: W. W. Norton, 1978), p. 7. The image of an indolent Hawthorne in the Custom House is one that Exley holds dear in *A Fan's Notes* and with which he thoroughly identifies. "Because these pages had begun to form themselves in my mind, the parallel

[between himself and Hawthorne] that I most cherished was his Custom House description of the languor which prevented him . . . from sitting down to write *The Scarlet Letter*" (p. 367).

13. C. Barry Chabot argues convincingly in "The Alternative Vision of Frederick Exley's *A Fan's Notes*" (*Critique*, 19 [1977], 87–100) that Exley's is one of the few American novels of recent years which conspicuously implicates its protagonist in the condemnation of American society that it offers, proving him to be contributory to the problems he himself decries.

14. Exley points to a similar author-character split in Edmund Wilson's *Memoirs of Hecate County* as he is discussing that work in his sequel to *A Fan's Notes*, *Pages from a Cold Island*. "Wilson deplored the notion of this work being autobiographical," Exley explains, "but in his concluding section, 'Mr. and Mrs. Blackburn at Home,' he'd invited such speculation by having his narrator write, 'In those days, what with revery and alcohol I carried so much of dreaming into real life and so much of my real life into dreams—as I have sometimes done in telling these stories—that I was not always quite sure which was which.' " *Pages from a Cold Island* (New York: Random House, 1975), p. 4.

15. Roger Sale, "Tying It Up," *The New York Review of Books* (June 26, 1975), p. 37.

16. Jorge Luis Borges, "Tlön, Uqbar, Orbis Tertius," trans. James E. Irby, in *Labyrinths* (New York: New Directions, 1964), p. 13.

17. One final example of the disparity between Frederick's narrative and Exley's might be offered here. Bumpy sends Frederick a "horny bestseller" and directs him to page 113, where he will find "a guy diving in bush." Believing that the book he is writing has no page-by-page coherence, Frederick never suspects that the best seller in question is the book he is writing, in which we find, on page 113, Frederick imagining that he is "diving in bush." Unhappily, however, this convergence works only in the Ballantine Books edition (1969), which is no longer in print.

18. The Ballantine Books edition italicized the fact that the "About the Author" blurb was to be considered part of the novel by printing "The End" beneath it. Noteworthy too is the fact that the blurb contains information abut Exley ("in 1948 he was unanimously selected for the north Westchester Interscholastic League basketball team") which contradicts portions of the portrait the novel offers, thus providing further evidence for the Frederick/Exley distinction.

19. Exley, *Pages from a Cold Island*, p. iii.

Barth, *Letters*, and the Great Tradition

Max F. Schulz
University of Southern California

i. *The Great Tradition*

Cervantes laughed away the self-important Chivalry of Spain with his creation of a single-minded, tunnel-visioned knight-errant for all time; Barth has just finished laughing away the self-reflexive Modernists of the twentieth century with his conception of an epistolary novel comprising eighty-eight letters, whose seven correspondents, all but one "reborn" from his previous books, self-consciously circle back upon the first half of their fictional existences, assiduously rewriting their lives to fit the new perspective of their mature years. With *LETTERS* Barth demonstrates that the creative self-questionings of *Lost in the Funhouse* and of *Chimera* are behind him. Besides being a self-reflexive novel meant to end all further attempts in that mode, *LETTERS* is an ambitious recreation of Barth's *oeuvre* to date, of the national mood of the late sixties, and of America's mythic sense of itself since its founding. Three of the letter writers are old acquaintances: Ambrose Mensch, Todd Andrews, and Jacob Horner. Two are the most recent scions of fictional ancestors: Andrew Burlingame Cook VI and Jerome Bonaparte Bray. One is newly created: Germaine Pitt, Lady Amherst, who is romantically and/or sexually involved to lesser or greater degree with all but Andrews and Horner; and one is newly recycled: "The Author"/Barth, who is incestuously involved, so to speak, with all these products of his own mind.

The sublime fusion of fact and fiction, life and art, of *LETTERS* is underscored by the novelist Barth including not only himself as "the Author" but also a third self in the alter-ego Ambrose, a fictitious dreamer of fictional plots that tend like Barth's to be avant-garde (cf. pp. 646–56).[1] The latter two carry on an epistolary exchange of advice about the writing of fiction, which looks hard (but optimistically) at what Barth is seeking to achieve with the novel in which they appear as

95

characters. In his final "Letter to the Author," Ambrose outlines for his friend and writing mentor a projected "old-time epistolary novel by seven fictitious drolls & dreamers . . . " (p. 769), which is a recapitulation of the novel Barth has just completed by that Letter. (The penultimate and ultimate Letters are not strictly part of the story: one is an alphabetical wedding toast sent two weeks earlier by "the Author" to Ambrose, and the other "the Author's" epistolary Envoi to the Reader.)[2] Ambrose's Letter, comprising seven paragraph clusters, with each cluster summarizing the "traditional letter-symbolism" of one of the first seven letters of the alphabet, represents Ambrose's "Farewell to formalism" (p. 768). More importantly, this formalist retraction masks (with its alphabetical masquerade) a less than fictitious, and less than facetious summary of how Barth sees his achievement at the midpoint in his writing career. It defines the outer limits of his literary ambition, and pinpoints his place in the Great Tradition. Generalizing in the letter "C" cluster on the meaning of *Conflict* as it has figured in his life and as it figures in the story he is outlining, Ambrose allegorizes (p. 767) his love affair with Lady Amherst thus:

> last-ditch provincial Modernist wishes neither to repeat nor to repudiate career thus far; wants the century under his belt but not on his back. *Complication*: he becomes infatuated with, enamored of, possessed by a fancied embodiment (among her other, more human, qualities and characteristics) of the Great Tradition and puts her—and himself—through sundry more or less degrading trials, which she suffers with imperfect love and patience, she being a far from passive lady, until he loses his cynicism and his heart to her spirited dignity and, at the *climax*, endeavors desperately, hopefully, perhaps vainly, to get her one final time with child: his, hers, theirs. (cc: Author)

The main plot of *LETTERS* is concerned with the quirky regional Maryland writer Ambrose's determination to beget a child on the middle-aged Anglo-French scholar-critic Lady Amherst. In their ultimate fruitful coupling, Barth makes explicit in *LETTERS* (what he had hesitantly and parodically broached in *The Sot-Weed Factor*) his bid to be considered more than just another contemporary writer of academic and avant-garde books—to be reckoned with as a twentieth-century novelist who is the distinguished heir to a proud centuries-long tradition of Anglo-American fiction. "Dear dignified Germaine," Ambrose addresses Lady Amherst in his first letter to her: "let us be lovers! . . . Muse of Austen, Dickens, Fielding, Richardson, and the rest: reclaim your prodigal! Speak love to me, Mother Tongue! O Britannia, your lost colony is reconquered!" (p. 41).[3] Securing his place among the great English realists of the eighteenth and nineteenth centuries, however, is not the end to Barth's aspirations. In his determined rehearsal of present and past national history as a parable of its own problematic ontology,[4] and in his postmodernist bent for self-transcendent parody[5] of past fictional forms, in *LETTERS*, he means to claim his place among the great global novelists who trace their lineage back to *Don Quixote*.

How seriously are we to take Barth's royal pretensions to historic literary legitimacy? An answer to that question has been made easier to get at with Barth's submission of *LETTERS* as his main credential in support of his kinship with fiction's aristocracy. To deal critically with *LETTERS* is to measure not just the boundaries of one novel but to pace off the whole back forty of Barth's fictional efforts, since the novel brings to full fruition the self-reflexive experimentation of *Lost in the Funhouse* and *Chimera*, and the parodic exercises of *The Sot-Weed Factor* and *Giles Goat-Boy*. Equally important the characters and plots of his prior books are ambitiously sifted, replanted, and harvested anew in this latest novel. They acquire antecedent and posterior histories, individual biographies growing into family sagas of generations.

The story of Ambrose's adolescent sexual stirrings and artistic yearnings (in *Lost in the Funhouse*) expands to include a Wolfean word-disgorgement about the Mensch family's modest contribution by way of their stonemason and construction business to the building and corruption of Maryland's Eastern Shore, particularly as embodied in the erection of Menschhaus. The contretemps of Ebenezer Cooke and Henry Burlingame III in the Indian wars and tobacco conspiracies of the late seventeenth-century Chesapeake Bay area (in *The Sot-Weed Factor*) are stretched across some eight more generations, bringing their heirs down to the present, adding a French-Canadian branch to the English-American and panoramically enlarging the field of the family's dedication to political counter-intelligence to include the Indian squabbles of the eighteenth century, the Old as well as the New worlds, and most of the major American and European wars of the eighteenth, nineteenth, and twentieth centuries, in the family's near global operations from the forests of the Northwest Territory and the courts of France and England to the island of St. Helena. Todd Andrews's affair with Jane Harrison in the 1930's (in *The Floating Opera*) is

replayed in 1969, and his then aborted suicide this time around successfully concluded against a backdrop of children and other lovers, po-
litical protesters, and the yachting community of the Chesapeake Bay.
At a shriller decibel level, the sordid life of Jacob Horner (in *The End of
the Road*) is extended to embrace the drug and commune delirium of
the sixties; and the sinister opera buffa rampages of the Bray clan (in
Giles Goat-Boy) are moved to an upstate New York pig farm Comalot
(The Kennedy years Camelot as perceived through the euphorium of a
Honey Dust induced haze) where the latest descendent Jerome
Bonaparte Bray computer-programs himself into an uncertain future.

Barth has managed the considerable Balzacian feat of containing the
fact and the function, the immediate and the historical—the
mythopoeic reality of America's nationhood, its dreams, traumas, and
guilty nightmares—all within one fat novel. To give a semblance of
order to these disparate materials he has borrowed from the "former
formalist" Ambrose (p. 769) an alphabetical and numerological design
(partly and originally "the Author's" own spelled out by him in a letter
to Ambrose of August 3, 1969 [pp. 654–55]), based on the number
seven: seven correspondents, one for each of his seven books (including
the one underway), in seven months of correspondence; seven separate
periods in Ambrose's erotic life with a comparable seven in his affair
with Lady Amherst; seven integers in the word Letters, as also in the
word Numbers, the working title and substance of a rival book Bray is
composing on the computer. Meshed with this design is another of
doubling every action. *Re-enactment* Barth calls it, and with this key
organizational device we move away from suspicious self-indulgent
formalist games toward an essential thematic order in the novel and in
Barth's creative perception of human experience.

ii. *The Recombinant Novel*

Barth likes to remind people that he is an opposite-sex twin. He also
likes to hint at the underlying significance of this genetic fact for his
fiction.[6] Analogously, he delights in toying with the epistemological
idea that the motive power of his fiction draws on the physical laws
governing mathematical computations and computer programming,
even as he is developing a parallel biological ontology. The twin energy
systems are first put to work in *Giles Goat-Boy*, followed up by *Lost in
the Funhouse*. In the latter, Barth continues to hoax many readers into
believing the key to that book's riddle lies in the business of the

moebius strip and tape recorder, when the life of the book dwells in the double growth (*Bildungs* and *Künstler*) of Ambrose as individual and as author. In *LETTERS* Barth continues the game, opposing the letters of "the Author" to the numbers of Jerome Bray. Despite all the arithmetical business—the Base-6 pattern of Ambrose ("sixes are *my* thing," p. 652; see pp. 761–64) and Base-7 of "the Author" and of Bray (he too gives the history of his world, its microchemical, literary, and astronomical phases in units of seven, designed to spawn a new generation of computer issued isomorphs, see pp. 755–58)—no one can mistake where Barth's real attention lies in *LETTERS*. Spermatozoan, not digitalization, is Barth's key to life, and fiction. The unstated but no less evident pun on the sense of these numerical antics being at "sixes and sevens" implies as much.

The genetic coding of the double helix, its continual dividing and recombining of organisms provides us with a trope for the developmental pattern thematically informing the lives of the characters and ultimately the form of *LETTERS*. A microcosm of such patterning is the twisting "double" line of Cooks and Burlingames, each generation "alternating surnames through the line of their first-born sons" (p. 26), Andrew Burlingame Cooke III followed by Henry Cooke Burlingame IV, succeeded by Andrew Burlingame Cooke IV, after which the name becomes plain Cook and "the male-primogenitural restriction" is dropped out of deference to "the splendid women of the Casteenes" (p. 26) to include Andrée's and Henrietta's, down to the living A. B. Cook VI and H. C. Burlingame VII. The helixical interchange of successive generations is matched by a correspondent family fidelity to political intrigue and uncertain fealty to the Indian strain in their blood. Each generation honors "his grandsire as a fail'd visionary, whilst dishonoring his sire as a successful hypocrite" (p. 280), and then in midlife separating from that line of development to create a new reverse coil of existence "correcting . . . life's first half" (p. 631; see p. 323). A further pattern stitching together the history of the two genetically interlocked families into new forms that are reduplicative of the past is summarized in Todd Andrews's offhand remark that "A. B. Cooks live in the past . . . and H. C. Burlingames in the future" (p. 88). Thus do the Cooks-Burlingames trace down through the centuries a recurrent design of doubling back on themselves, repeated at the psychological level of father pitted against son in the Freudian generational "compulsion to repeat" (p. 636) old errors.

What one gets in each of the six life stories told—Ambrose Mensch's, Lady Amherst's, Todd Andrews's, Jacob Horner's, Jerome Bray's, and A. B. Cook's-H. C. Burlingame's (IV–VI and IV–VII)—is revised life cycle, Barth's asseverations of his fictive intentions to the contrary, rather than mechanical reiteration. Biological growth that genetically recalls, but does not duplicate, the old pattern more accurately describes the narrative process of *LETTERS* than does re-enactment. All six fictive letter writers at some point in the novel address their old selves in a resumé of the first half of their lives, which cites the changes having occurred to them and in that self-scrutiny contributes to the on-going act of self-recreation.

The recurrent patterned twisting of the genetic code ("Every text implies a counter-text," p. 534) supplies the creative act—sexual/ biological and imaginative/artful—with an underlying *topos* on which Barth grounds even such nonbiological and nonverbal variants on growth as the cellulose world of cinema and the mathematical logic of the computer. The Reg Prinz filming of Barth's "last book"—which simultaneously includes *Lost in the Funhouse* and the "Ongoing Latest . . . even [to] such projected works as *LETTERS*" (p. 192)—is an helixical spin-off in a new form of the entire novel, as is also Jerome Bray's computer programmed effort to offset *LETTERS* with "the world's 1st work of Numerature" (p. 527). Each presents an alternative sign system to that of print as a solution to the postmodernist crisis in communication. Both, furthermore, blur the interface between real and make-believe. Prinz incorporates the ongoing romance of Ambrose and Lady Amherst, and the 1960's protest movements, into his film of Barth's prior fiction; while Bray, playing the part of a libidinous *Rex Numerator* to what he punningly calls Barth's "King Author," keeps recruiting "real life" equivalents to be his royal (and blessed) consort *Regina de Nominatrix*:

> To sit at his right hand at the Table of Multiplication, play Ordinate to his Abscissa, share the Pentagonal Bed, receive his innumerable seed, make royal jelly, and bring forth numerous golden heirs. (p. 638)

Finally, out of the organisms of his past novels "the Author"/Barth is regenerating a new novel, *LETTERS*, which is the child of the second half of his literary career. Thus does "the Author"/Barth also engage, like his six fictive correspondents, in self-recreation in the changing form of his fiction, which is the only "life" finally important to a writer.

The most complex genetic exchange involves the intertwining double helix of *AmB*rose (AB) and "the *A*uthor"/*B*arth (AB). The fictional creation of Barth in *Lost in the Funhouse*, Ambrose now supplies "the Author"/Barth with the Perseus and Bellerophon tales, "both concerning midlife crises and Second Cycles that echo First" (p. 652), so Barth can write a sixth book *Chimera*, thus making it possible for him to complete the Base-7 structure of *LETTERS* by its being "Opus # 7" (p. 652). In gratitude "the Author"/Barth responds:

> Time was when you and I were so close in our growings-up and literary apprenticeships, so alike in some particulars and antithetical in others, that we served each as the other's alter ego and aesthetic conscience; eventually even as the other's fiction. (p. 653)

The twists of their deoxyribonucleic codes are intertwined in *LET-TERS* so that they share—with some sleight-of-hand reversal of authorial roles and identities—responsibility for conception of the novel and for part of the epistolary exchange within the novel. Technically and aesthetically their respective careers as fictionists evolve along parallel yet contrary coiling lines like the skeins of a braid. Ambrose the "former formalist" (p. 769) of *Chimera* inspiration turns realist, writes the linear saga of the Mensch family, and then swears off writing forever; while the Barth of early realistic stories set on the Maryland Eastern Shore acquires the credentials of a SUNY Buffalo avant-garde writing teacher bent on concocting an ultra formalist novel called *LET-TERS* which he hopes will auspiciously inaugurate the second half of his career.

The intertwined DNA of Ambrose and Barth—the A and B building blocks, fictional and factual, formalist and realist, creative code of *LETTER*'s life—is underscored by the pervasive alphabet-letter play worked into the novel. This letter-play is probably more consequential symbolically for our understanding of Barth's profound appraisal of a writer's cultural role as an analogue of the original, and continuing, cosmic creation of things than thematically for our grasp of his organization of *LETTERS*. Barth has shown partiality in his novels to a limited range of names (for example, *Andrew*: Andrew Cooke, Todd Andrews, André and Andrée Castine) restricted to the initial letters of the alphabet. The most arresting, of course, are the A. B. Cooks (ABC) who with the H. C. Burlingames (H[āch]CB) in some sense form the original nucleic acid of Barth's creative imagination. But the back-up

company of characters who seem to be trapped similarly at the beginning of the alphabet is considerable: the alternating generations of
Henri and André (or Andrée) Casteenes, the Ahatchwhoops Chicamec
and Cohunkowprets, John Coode, the Brays, Merope Bernstein, Bea
Golden, Marsha Blank, and Lady Amherst ("my 'Lady A,' " p. 53), as
well as such historical personages as Bonaparte, Admirals Cockrane and
Cockburn, Aaron Burr, and innumerable others stuck at the letters A,
B, and C. Then there is the intriguing link-up of John Barth (JB) with
those antithetical other JB's, Joel Barlow and Jerome Bray, both em-
bodiments, one historical and the other fictional, of the antithetical
twists of DNB which make up the social continuum of savior and pa-
riah. It has to do, no doubt, with Barth's own name—"bee-beta-beth,
the Kabbalist's letter of Creation, whence derived, like life itself from
the marsh primordial, both the alphabet and the universe it described
by its recombinations" (p. 47)—and with most of these creatures being
the deoxyribonucleic offshoots of his own brain waves; but it also has to
do with Barth's perception of the propaedeutic importance of words not
only to the identity of an individual but also to the recombinative
powers of the writer, and, through him, the vitality and health of the
community.

iii. *The Great American Novel*

A major novel must be rooted in the native soil of its language and
in the cultural zone of its time. Only then can its author, assuming he
has a large ambition, hope to transcend the limitations of the local
scene, with his novel about a specific region and society ultimately
yielding universal insights about the human venture. There is no mis-
taking that Barth intends us to take *LETTERS* seriously as a heavy-
weight contender for the Great Tradition. And many of its early reviewers who were most positive have done just that—although grudg-
ingly and gracelessly, irritated with him for serving up such an indi-
gestible lump. They sensed its greatness and hesitated to denigrate its
ingredients, yet found the mixture unpalatable and too obsessed with
its own textures and flavors. This is perhaps because a novel clamoring
to be ranked as a great realistic portrayal of the American experience is
also parading itself as a parody of its own self-referential impulse. As if
this is not enough self-contradiction, *LETTERS* appears long after the-
orists of the novel have dismissed realism as an anachronism and the
idea of the Great American Novel as an impossibility, if not an imper-

tinence. All of which leaves us unprepared aesthetically and psychologically to digest our good fortune.

In the aftermath of the Civil War, Whitman's 1855 call for a poet who would embody the national aspirations had reached ready ears. For the rest of the century and into the first three decades of ours were heard disappointed laments that the Great American Novel "is yet unwritten."[7] It was not for want of trying. By the 1920's and 30's, though, a weariness and even cynicism with the idea set in. These are the years of William Carlos Williams's feeble recipe for *The Great American Novel* (1923) and of Clyde Brion Davis's quizzical pretense at *"The Great American Novel—"* (1938)—which reveal a general loss of confidence in the whole idea. With the 1940's the almost century-old myth of the Great American Novel had spent itself, supplanted by a rebellious generation's counterstrain that "the novel was dead." Most recently Philip Roth has trivialized the idea in his Black Humor baseball story *The Great American Novel* (1973).

Yet, here is *LETTERS*, a novel which unabashedly claims our attention, in part, for its synthesis of the structural and post-structural concerns with linguistic indeterminacy and partial object and, in part, for its mythopoeic assimilation of the national self-image as being a manifest destiny of rebellion and counter-rebellion. It is not surprising, then, that early readers of *LETTERS*, somewhat puzzled and uncertain of its intentions, have tagged it an "epic of the American sensibility" but more an *Anarchaid* than *Aeneid*,[8] and a "quirky, wasteful, fascinating thing" that is "a work of genius whether one likes it or not."[9]

Whitman envisioned a great national poet whose spirit would incarnate "his country's spirit . . . its geography and national life and rivers and lakes,"[10] This is an elemental formula fitted to a pioneering nation still solving the problems of assimilating vast tracts of diverse wilderness and of uniting north, south, east and west. In the hundred years following Whitman's call the requisites for the Great American Novel grew in number, complexity, and sophistication. It must incorporate the American dream(s) of frontier egalitarianism, democratic individualism, and the rags-to-riches success of the self-made man. It must honor the American peculiarities of solitude and rootlessness. It must personify the themes of initiation and of the journey from innocence to knowledge. It must accommodate the new man emancipated from the old world burden of history and the celibate wanderer aloof

from society. It must reflect in its form the dynamic openness, constant
growth, and perpetual permutations of the American society.
Discussants in this century have argued that both "Palefaces" and
"Redskins" must make room around the campfire "cult of experience"
for the intellectual;[11] and the active continent tamer and practical
business manager similarly must allow the aesthetic dreamer and idler
to come out of his introspective closet. Finally, with the coming of literary self-consciousness in this century, the Great American Novel
must combine the realistic conventions of the nineteenth-century novel
with the self-reflexive techniques of the twentieth. It must encompass
the historical experiences of taming a wilderness and of creating a nation out of diverse national and ethnic groups; and at the same time it
must convey the preoccupations of the twentieth century with the indeterminacy of form and language, the mystique of signs, and the challenge of cinema, television, and visual image. Last of all, it must simultaneously be topical and recondite, avant-garde and conservative.

Such an awesome conglomerate of items would make even the wiz-
ards of *la nouvelle cuisine* hesitate; yet *LETTERS* manages to combine
them more convincingly and winsomely than any American novel to
date. That this has been a deliberate and conscious effort on Barth's
part is evident in his remarks during the 1978 Writer's Symposium
held at the University of Cincinnati. "I have at times," he confessed to
John Hawkes,

> gone farther than I want to go in the direction of a fiction that foregrounds
> language and form, displacing the ordinary notion of content, of
> "aboutness." But beginning with the "Chimera" novellas—written after the
> "Lost in the Funhouse" series, where that foregrounding reaches its peak or
> its nadir, depending on your esthetic—I have wanted my stories to be *about*
> things: about the passions, which Aristotle tells us are the true subject of
> literature. I'm with Aristotle on that. Of course form can be passionate; lan-
> guage itself can be passionate. These are not the passions of the viscera, but
> that doesn't give them second-class citizenship in the republic of the
> passions. More and more, as I get older, I nod my head yes to Aristotle. I
> want my fictions to be not only passionately formal, not only passionately
> "in the language," as Theodore Roethke used to say about poems he liked,
> but passionately about things in life as well. That I think I'm achieving;
> simplicity maybe not.[12]

LETTERS successfully blends the Maryland-based realism of *The End of
the Road* and *The Floating Opera* with the self-reflexive and formalist

concerns about the creative act itself of *Lost in the Funhouse* and *Chimera*. As more than one reviewer of *LETTERS* observed, "the best run[s] of sustained writing" record Todd Andrews's cruise along the Eastern Shore and up the rivers of the Chesapeake Bay,[13] the Mensch family's ruin as Eastern Shore stonemasons and general contractors,[14] and Ambrose Mensch's Rabelaisian courtship, by turns scandalous, scatologous, and scintillating, of Lady Amherst (as told by her). At the same time the special authorial relationship Barth contrives between himself and Ambrose ("old fellow toiler up the slopes of Parnassus" and "old altered ego," "the Author"/Barth lovingly addresses him, p. 655) establishes a frame of reference for the metafictional concerns Barth is so skilled at structuring into narrative form. In an important exchange of letters and telephone calls, between them on the subject of "the Author"/Barth's epistolary novel-in-progress ("the Author": August 3, 24; Ambrose: August 25, 1969) Barth generalizes on the folly of presuming the reality of "each of the several *LETTERS* correspondents, explicitly or otherwise" (p. 655). "Never mind," he writes Ambrose, "what your predecessors have come up with, and never mind that in a sense this 'dialogue' is a monologue; that we capital-A Authors are ultimately, ineluctably, and forever talking to ourselves. If our correspondence is after all a fiction, we like, we *need* that fiction: it makes our job less lonely" (p. 655). In his use of the word *fiction* in several of its senses—that which is nonfactual and nonexistent, and that which is an artistically contrived reality, an artifice mimetic of reality—Barth means to acknowledge "the modernist concern with the derangements of art, sex, and culture,"[15] and with the indeterminacy of signs, signifier, and signified; and to merge these verbal contingencies with a fictional world of definable peoples, places, and times.

In other words, the symbiosis of Ambrose and "the Author"/Barth signals the basic narrative design of *LETTERS*: at once formalist and realist. The novel is replete with individual instances of the desperate shifts of history and fiction to come to terms with language. Ambrose fancies himself a hero patterned after Lord Raglan's "biography of the typical mythic hero" (p. 646) and recycles himself in the second half of his life by fathering himself anew on Lady Amherst whom he invokes as "Fair Embodiment of the Great Tradition, of my keyless codes, my chain-letter narratives with missing links, my edible anecdotes, my action-fictions, my *récits concrets*, my tapes and slides and assemblages and *histoires trouvées*" (p. 39).

The English naval commander Lord Cockburn, who historically burned Washington, is portrayed as giving special attention to the demolition of the *National Intelligencer* and its printing presses, which "for two years has been abusing him in its columns" (p. 510). With its destruction he means to erase past unflattering accounts of himself; and, by also destroying all upper case C's among the type, to insure that no future ones will be printed. On a less negative note, Jerome Bray is forever resetting his computer program to produce mathematical fiction analogous to the base set of "the Author"/Barth's and of Reg Prinz's narrative strategies. Subsuming all of them is Barth's reduction of the events of *LETTERS* (the pasts of his characters in his previous books, and the pre and post Revolution history of America) into a *cinema verité*. The film is intended by its director Prinz, who despises words and speaks only in "ellipses, shrugs, nods, fragments, hums, non sequiturs, dashes, and suspension points" (p. 218), to recover "the visual purity [and inarticulation] of silent movies" (p. 223). Its climax is the 1812 sack of Washington, which Prinz wishes to commemorate microcosmically in the burning of the Library of Congress, thereby recording not only the destruction of an historical city "but the venerable metropolis of letters" (p. 233). During the filming of this event Prinz also makes a homicidal attempt on Ambrose's life (his "too wordy" scriptwriter, pp. 65, 224) by pushing over "an eight-foot case of 'books' (actually painted rows of spines but the case itself . . . a heavy wooden thing)" with the intention of its falling on him. Ambrose retaliates by beaning Prinz with "Richardson's novel" (p. 663).

The nervous modernist thrust of *LETTERS*, hyped-up and self-mocking, is offset by its realistic accommodation of the sixties political protest movements, sexual revolution, and minority demands. Firmly positioning the novel in the American present the scenes of social unrest further are anchored in the fathoms deep waters of American diplomatic and military history. The War of 1812 (itself a re-enactment of the American Revolution) is dimly echoed by the Vietnam War; the Indian Conspiracies of Joseph Brant, Pontiac, and Tecumseh by the civil rights activities of Drew Mack; the London-Paris-Algerine diplomacies of Joel Barlow by the Niagara-Chesapeake Bay legal consultancies of Todd Andrews. Above all, the multi-generational saga of the Cook-Burlingame-Casteene clan takes us from the late seventeenth to late twentieth centuries, embracing enroute much of the conspiratorial history of the American colonial and federal governmental intrigues with the Indians of the Eastern Americas and the governments of England and France. In the successive members of the Cook-Burlingame-Casteene family Barth embodies most of the distinctive qualities identified as part of the American experience and requisite for the Great American Novel. The sweep of geography covered is equally impressive: from the Great Lakes to the Louisiana bayous, from the Tidewater lands to the Mississippi River, with full loving recreations of the Chesapeake Bay islands and inlets and of the Buffalo-Niagara-Ontario area.

One can think of no American novel seizing "the pen of History" (p. 750) that covers as much American territory and history as *LETTERS*. Missing are the slavery and abolition troubles of the south, and the westward movement into the great plains, southwest deserts, and northwest forests. Rather than risk diffusion of a remarkably tight plot, and risk loss of a convincing sense of place, Barth has wisely left the freeing of the American blacks to Styron's *The Confessions of Nat Turner*, Haley's *Roots*, and Reed's *Flight to Canada*; and the winning of the west to Guthrie's *Big Sky*, Berger's *Little Big Man*, and Michener's *Centennial*.

iv. *The Great Recombinant American Postmodernist Tradition*

LETTERS is at once a novel of historical fact and of contrived fiction. Like such other recent novels as Coover's *Public Burning* and Doctorow's *Ragtime* with similar authorial ambitions toward embodying the American psyche, *LETTERS* strives to embrace a Zeitgeist in which the documentary rivals fabulation in strangeness and interest. There is the difference that in addition to historical personages and imagined figures, *LETTERS* includes individuals who claim to be the real-life models for characters in Barth's previous novels. These levels of reality, which are bent on "muddling . . . the distinction between Art and Life" (p. 51), strive to contain the relevant and the universal.

In this regard, *LETTERS* is an unsettling mix of international novelistic forms and avant-garde formalist and mixed-media means. Ostensibly an epistolary novel, it mocks the conventional form such novels took under Richardson's lead. The sorely besieged eighteenth-century damsel warding off sexual assaults with her left hand while recording them to a pen pal with the right is transfigured by Barth into Lady Amherst, a fortyish literary scholar, who chronicles her marathon sexual bouts with Ambrose Mensch in prose that irrepressibly celebrates her dual insatiable sexual and scriblerian appetites:

Thus our gluttony persists, to my astonishment, into its fourth week! I should not have believed either my endurance or my appetite: I've easily done more coupling in the month of April than in the four years past; must have swallowed half as much as I've envaginated; I do not even count what's gone in the ears, up the arse, on the bedclothes and nightclothes and dayclothes and rugs and furniture, to the four winds. And yet I hunger and thirst for more: *my left hand creeps sleeping-himward as the right writes on*; now I've an instrument in each, poor swollen darling that I must have again. He groans, he stirs, he rises; my faithful English Parker pen (bought in "Mr. Pumblechook's premises," now a stationer's, in Rochester, in honour of great Boz) must yield to his poky poking pencil pencel pinced penicellus penicillus *peeee*

(pp. 70–71; my italics except for the last word quoted)

LETTERS belongs in the company of such counter-genre novels as *Don Quixote* which masquerade in the form they are mocking. The parallel with Cervantes's novel is profound. Little more than fifty years after the appearance of the first picaresque novel, *Lazarillo de Tormes* (1554), *Don Quixote* (1605) brilliantly uses the pseudo-autobiographical convention of the rogue hero as an ironical commentary on both literary and historical experience by recasting "the [picaresque] narrator's individual and willfully limited point of view"[16] (an essentially literary embrace of experience) into an historical context with a "second" consciousness, the author's, extrinsic to the sequence of events. It thus works, in Aristotelian terms, a "crucial *rapprochement* between literature and history—to the organization and detailed recreation and tolerant understanding of the concrete wealth of experience by a 'third' person,"[17] the reader.

Barth has played a similar counter-generic turn on the epistolary-confessional novels of the last two hundred years, which is even more appropriate than Cervantes's sophistication of the picaresque novel for the "*rapprochement* between literature and history," given the ironic distancing of events by successive consciousnesses in the writer-reader relationship, and given the diachronic nature of the epistolary convention. Barth sets forth his grasp of these implications intrinsic to the kind of novel he is about to write in his opening Letter "to the Reader" dated "March 2, 1969":

Gentles all: *LETTERS* is now begun . . .

If "now" were the date above, I should be writing this from Buffalo, New York, on a partly sunny Sunday mild for that area in that season, when Lake Erie is still frozen and the winter's heaviest snowfall yet ahead. On the 61st day of the 70th year of the 20th century of the Christian calendar, the human world and its American neighborhood, having survived, in the main, the shocks of "1968" and its predecessors . . .

But every letter has two times, that of its writing and that of its reading, which may be so separated, even when the post office does its job, that very little of what obtained when the writer wrote will still when the reader reads. And to the units of epistolary fictions yet a third time is added: the actual date of composition, which will not likely correspond to the letter-head date, a function more of plot or form than of history. It is *not* March 2, 1969: when I began this letter it was October 20, 1973: an inclement Tuesday morning in Baltimore, Maryland. The Viet Nam War was "over"; its peacemakers were honored with the Nobel Prize; the latest Arab-Israeli war, likewise "over" . . .

Now it's not 10/30/73 any longer, either. In the time between my first setting down "March 2, 1969" and now, "now" has become January 1974. Nixon won't go away; neither will the "energy crisis" or inflation-plus-recession . . .

The plan of *LETTERS* calls for a second Letter to the Reader at the end of the manuscript, by when what I've "now" recorded will seem already as remote as "March 2, 1969." By the time *LETTERS* is print, ditto for what shall be recorded in that final letter. And—to come at last to the last of a letter's times—by the time *your* eyes, Reader, review these epistolary fictive *a*'s-to-*z*'s, the "United States of America" may be setting about its Tri- or Quadricentennial, or be still floundering through its Bi-, or be a mere memory . . . (pp. 42–45)

As suggested by the historical references, much excised in this quotation, Barth, like Cervantes in his confrontation with an antiquated cultural heritage, has put American history under the multiple lens of an "Action Historiography" (p. 750) of factual and fictive perspectives.

It is as if Barth has taken literally Whitman's vision of the past animating the present and, vice versa, of the present reconstituting the past—a comprehensive viewpoint reinforced by Borges's notion of the literary enterprise, which we know Barth admires. The great poet, Whitman insisted, must join past, present, and future, forming "the consistence of what is to be from what has been and is. He drags the dead out of their coffins and stands them again on their feet . . . . he says to the past, Rise and walk before me that I may realize you. He learns the lesson . . . . he places himself where the future becomes present."[18] *The Sot-Weed Factor* was a tentative (if one will allow the use of such a term for such a fat assertive tome) start for Barth in this direction, which bothered more than one critic because of his seeming pointless parody of the eighteenth-century English novel. With *LET-TERS* we can now see what he was feeling his way toward all this time, for the novel dismisses a cherished literary fetish that sustained a century of American writers fiercely resentful of the seeming impoverished American social scene and the overpowering European literary tradition.

In *The Great American Novel* (1923) William Carlos Williams hurled a diatribe against the continuing Old World domination of American literature.

> America is a mass of pulp, a jelly, a sensitive plate ready to take whatever print you want to put on it—We have no art, no manners, no intellect—We have nothing . . . We have only movement like a sea. But we are not a sea—[19]

Williams's 1923 curveball against America followed by roughly fifty years the more famous indictment by Henry James of a nonexistent American culture. Now another fifty years have passed and an American author has managed to do what James and Williams deplored as beyond their means. Nor has he done it as Williams imagined to be the only way possible, by freeing the language from the European tradition ("The background of America is not Europe but America"; "Every word we get must be broke off from the European mass")[20] so words could resonate with a sense of a *"Nuevo Mundo* on which white feet before Columbus's and his crews had never walked."[21]

The European literary tradition which James and Williams found so heady, and so pernicious for their native grain, Barth treats as a "poetics" manipulable to his local and global purposes. With bold imagination he presses the epistolary mode of the Richardson novel into service as a sensibility through which to refract the diplomatic history of the fledgling United States. In the process he absorbs other historical and fictive epistolary exercises in sentiment: Madame de Stael's letters edited by Lady Amherst, the "notorious John Henry Letters" (p. 110) authored by the Cook-Burlingames masquerading as European statesmen, and the "transcension of conventional forms, including the conventional categories of art and social class," in the "sentiment and sensation" confessional "novel-in-letters, *The Sorrows of Werther"* (p. 283) innovated by Goethe. The consequence is an ironic recreation of American history as a moveable domestic drama of individuals and their star-crossed amours. The principal set of "love letters" in the novel is penned by Lady Amherst, who despite her protestations represents for "the Author"/Barth "the Great Tradition" (p. 57). Her letters detail her venturous union with the enigmatic New World figure André Casteene (alias A. B. Cook VI—or vice versa) to conceive the revolutionary "New Leftist" H. C. Burlingame VII; and then in mid-career her coupling with Ambrose to coax new life out of the exhausted paradigms of her aging uterus ("half-century-old womb," p. 760) and his "low motile sperm" (p. 64). As "Literature Incarnate, or The Story Thus Far," she is mother to both "the pen of History" (p. 750) and the "next turning" of literature, which Ambrose has "aspired to have a hand in" (p. 40).

LETTERS is literally the product of those two unions: at once the revolutionary history of America by way of the genealogically inspired letters of A. B. Cook IV and VI; and the literary history of its own engendering by way of the conceptually inspired epistles of Lady Amherst, Ambrose, and "the Author"/Barth. To realize a secondary "objective" perspective on the events narrated by the Cooks and by Amherst-Ambrose, Barth asks the reader to digest them anew as ironic "historical" and "artful" constructs of the 1960's American consciousness: by way of the frame actions of the campus and political protest movements and of Reg Prinz's filming of Barth's fiction. The subject of the Great American Novel becomes then, in part, a regeneration of historical and literary pasts and, in part, a self-conscious witness to this regeneration. It is a story about the writing of the story of the American past, present, and future.

In 1967 Barth wrote an influential article on "The Literature of Exhaustion."[22] This past year he updated his idea of twentieth-century fiction with a second article on "The Literature of Replenishment: Post-modernist Fiction." By a "literature of replenishment" Barth means one that "is the synthesis or transcension of . . . premodernist and modernist modes of writing."

> If the modernists, carrying the torch of romanticism, taught us that linearity, rationality, consciousness, cause and effect, naive illusionism, transparent language, innocent anecdote, and middle-class moral conventions are not the whole story, then from the perspective of these closing decades of our century we may appreciate that the contraries of these things are not the whole story either. Disjunction, simultaneity, irrationalism, anti-illusionism, self-reflexiveness, medium-as-message, political olympianism,

and a moral pluralism approaching moral entropy—these are not the whole story either.

"The Literature of Exhaustion," it now appears, was "really about . . . the effective 'exhaustion' not of language or of literature but of the aesthetic of high modernism." The "simple burden" of that essay "was that the forms and modes of art live in human history and are therefore subject to used-upness, at least in the minds of significant numbers of artists in particular times and places; in other words, that artistic conventions are liable to be retired, subverted, transcended, transformed, or even deployed against themselves to generate new and lively work."[23] If the new literature of replenishment turns out to sound a lot like a revisionist updating of the literature of exhaustion that should not surprise us, especially when viewed in the light of the helixical progression of subject and form (he has observed that his novels come in pairs)[24] in Barth's fictional career to date. And if the postmodernist synthesis of eighteenth- and nineteenth-century realism with twentieth-century modernism seems uncannily to describe LETTERS, that too is an exercise in literary self-definition and critical hindsight authors are privileged to practice.

All these reduplicative processes are seen by Barth to have coalesced in the late sixties. According to him 1969 was not only "a vintage year" for the French wine-growers association (p. 44) but also for the Great Recombinant American Postmodernist Novel. That is the year he epistolarily dates as the start of his writing LETTERS, to be precise March 2nd, or—in a gesture of fidelity to the numerological structure of the novel—"On the 61st day of the 70th year" (p. 42). And the novel arrests its restructuring of American history at that date, even though admitting that other subsequent times—those of its writing (actually begun October 30, 1973) and of its reading—will bring later points of view to bear on these events. LETTERS is thus the *trompe l'oeil* of all this nationalistic and belle-lettristic ending and beginning: (1) The revolutionary and counter-revolutionary impulses of America and Europe the past three hundred years and the radical and counter-reactive movements of the 1960's have combined to initiate a new sexually liberated, politically activist, and self-consciously plural society. (2) The formal Aristotelian modes of the pre-twentieth-century European novel and the experimental fictional period of the Modernists have been merged to realize a new postmodernist form for that subject matter. (3) And the epistolary exchanges between Lady Amherst, Ambrose, et al. and "the Author"/Barth about the state of America and of American letters, and about the progress of *LETTERS*, has given imitative form to it all. Even though *LETTERS* has brought to closure one series of recombinant actions, it also figures as the nucleus for starting the loop of a new set of "happenings" and "understandings." So Barth's opening confession "to the Reader" of the long gestation period of the novel would have us believe; and so his theoretical summary in the 1967 and 1980 articles, of the ongoing reduplication of life and art from exhaustion to replenishment, works to reaffirm.

The unequivocal self-confidence of these remarks about the longevity of *LETTERS*, and about the form of the novel in the last quarter of the twentieth century, leaves unproblematical the future in Barth's eyes of his novel. It is meant by its author to take a lead position among postmodernist novels with such other pacesetters as Italo Calvino's *Cosmicomics* (1965) and Gabriel Garcia Marquez's *One Hundred Years of Solitude* (1967), both of which Barth cites as worthy competitors.[25] And it is to be numbered among those great novels of the past, whose formal synthesis of the traditional and the innovative has summed up periods of human history. Here is his roll-call of the company and the tradition he aspires to:

> Anticipations of the "postmodernist literary aesthetic" have duly been traced through the great modernists of the first half of the twentieth century—T. S. Eliot, William Faulkner, André Gide, James Joyce, Franz Kafka, Thomas Mann, Robert Musil, Ezra Pound, Marcel Proust, Gertrude Stein, Miguel Unamuno, Virginia Woolf—through *their* nineteenth-century predecessors—Alfred Jarry, Gustave Flaubert, Charles Baudelaire, Stéphane Mallarmé, and E. T. A. Hoffman—back to Laurence Sterne's *Tristram Shandy* (1767) and Miguel Cervantes's *Don Quixote* (1615).[26]

"With *Don Quixote*," Barth observes, "the novel may be said to *begin* in self-transcendent parody." Cervantes managed his stunning narrative assimilation of Spanish social and literary histories using the picaresque tradition as his foil. With *LETTERS* Barth has created a novel in the same vein. It is an imitation (in the Coleridgean sense of the word), however, not a copy, using the narrative conventions of the past several centuries to establish on its own terms a fusion of the American experience and the Anglo-American-European epistolary and confessional novel tradition. It stands in its earned integrity as a twentieth-century literary milestone, as *Don Quixote* marks an earlier century, in the history of "transactions with individual readers over time, space, and language."[27]

NOTES

1. John Barth, *LETTERS* (New York: G. P. Putnam's Sons, 1979). Page references cited in the text are to this edition.

2. The latest dated letter, that of Todd Andrews's "Draft codicil" to his "Last Will & Testament," 26 September 1969, occurs nine pieces of writing from the end. In this "epistle" is buried the final action of the narrative: the imminent explosion of the Morgan Memorial Tower on the campus of Marshyhope State University, in which are presumably besides Andrews, Ambrose Mensch the self-conscious avant-gardist of language and form, Reg Prinz the film maker and despiser of words, and Jerome Bray the anti-language numerologist of the computer, all of whom will be blown to smithereens at sunrise 6:54 A.M.—the minute on which the narrative inconclusively stops.

3. But see Lady Amherst's riposte of April 5 to *"the Author"* (not to Ambrose who on March 3 had invoked her as "Muse of the Realistic Novel"), rejecting his invitation of March 23 to figure as a letter writer and fictional character ("my heroine, my creation," p. 53): "I am *not* Literature! I am *not* the Great Tradition! I am *not* the aging Muse of the Realistic Novel!" (p. 57).

4. The Phrase is Brian Stonehill's, in "A Trestle of *LETTERS*," *Fiction International*, 12 (1980), 263, apropos of the characters' lives in *LETTERS*.

5. So Barth characterizes *Don Quixote*, in "The Literature of Replenishment: Postmodernist Fiction," *The Atlantic*, 245 (January 1980), 71.

6. Barth most recently announced in discussion with John Hawkes during a Fiction Festival at the University of Cincinnati, 2 November 1978: "One day I realized to my delight (I'm an opposite-sex twin) that all my books come in pairs" ("Hawkes and Barth Talk About Fiction," *NYTBR*, April 1, 1979, p. 7).

7. T. S. Perry, "American Novels," *North American Review*, 115 (October 1872), 378.

8. Josephine Hendon, *"Letters*: A Novel by John Barth," *The New Republic*, 181 (December 1, 1979), 32.

9. Thomas R. Edwards, "A Novel of Correspondences," *NYTBR*, September 30, 1979, p. 33.

10. Walt Whitman, Preface to 1855 *Leaves of Grass*, in *The Collected Writings of Walt Whitman*, eds. Harold W. Blodgett and Sculley Bradley (New York: New York Univ. Press, 1965), p. 711.

11. Philip Rahv, *Image and Idea; Fourteen Essays on Literary Themes* (New York: New Directions, 1949), pp. 1–21. See also Leslie Fiedler, *Love and Death in the American Novel* (New York: Criterion, 1960; rev. ed., New York: Stein and Day, 1966); and Steven G. Kellman, *The Self-Begetting Novel* (New York: Columbia Univ. Press, 1980), pp. 101–28, whose review of the history of the American novel within the context of the self-begetting novel is richly suggestive.

12. "Hawkes and Barth Talk About Fiction," *NYTBR*, April 1, 1979, p. 32. In his most recent interview Barth discusses *LETTERS* in the context of "The Literature of Exhaustion" and of Modernism and Postmodernism, experimental and realistic storytelling; and ruminates on where he stands in relation to the changing novelistic form. *See* George Reilly, "An Interview with John Barth," *Contemporary Literature*, 22 (1981), 1–23.

13. Geoffrey Wolff, "Long Letters, Lost Liberty, Languid Love," *Esquire*, 92 (October 1979), 17.

14. Bejnamin DeMott, "Six Novels in Search of a Novelist," *The Atlantic*, 244 (November 1979), 92.

15. Hendon, p. 34.

16. Claudio Guillén, *Literature as System: Essays Toward the Theory of Literary History* (Princeton: Princeton Univ. Press, 1971), p. 156.

17. Ibid.

18. Whitman, Preface to 1855 *Leaves of Grass, Collected Writings of Walt Whitman*, eds. Blodgett and Bradley, p. 716. A little later in the essay Whitman rhapsodizes again on the need of the artist to recombine yesterday and today: "The direct trial of him who would be the greatest poet is today. If he does not flood himself with the immediate age as with vast oceanic tides . . . and if he be not himself the age transfigured . . . and if to him is not opened the eternity which gives similitude to all periods and locations and processes and animate and inanimate forms and which is the bond of time, and rises up from its inconceivable vagueness and infiniteness in the swimming shape of today. . . ."

19. William Carlos Williams, *The Great American Novel* (Paris: William Carlos Williams, 1923), p. 25.

20. Ibid., pp. 47, 26.

21. Ibid., p. 33.

22. John Barth, "The Literature of Exhaustion," *The Atlantic*, 220 (August 1967), 29–34.

23. Barth, "The Literature of Replenishment," *The Atlantic*, 245 (January 1980) 70–71.

24. "Hawkes and Barth Talk About Fiction," *NYTBR*, April 1, 1979, p. 7. As a follow-up to this observation, Barth mused, "I try to imagine in [my books] an organicity or continuity. It would be presumptuous to call it growth, but it certainly is related change" (p. 7).

25. Barth, "The Literature of Replenishment," pp. 70–71.

26. Ibid., p. 66.

27. Ibid., p. 71.

Comic Structure and the Double Time-Scheme of Hawkes's *Second Skin*

Donald R. Wineke
Wichita State University

In the 1964 interview that has become a cornerstone for recent critical appraisal of his work, John Hawkes declared that he began writing "on the assumption that the true enemies of the novel were plot, character, setting, and theme, and having once abandoned these familiar ways of thinking about fiction, totality of vision or structure was really all that remained."[1] Structure, defined as "verbal and psychological coherence," had supplanted the familiar conventions of fiction as his primary concern. At the same time, he acknowledged that *Second Skin* was his most conventional novel to date, adding that it was inspired partly by the need to parody that form.[2] Together, these statements provide us with a useful perspective on *Second Skin* by suggesting that he had at least two distinct but complementary purposes in writing it: on the one hand, to continue his experimentation with form as the manifestation of "verbal and psychological coherence," and, on the other, to exorcise the "true enemies of the novel" through parody.

However, it would, I think, be a mistake to make too much of the parody in *Second Skin*, to think of it in terms of parody alone.[3] The novel was also intended to be a comedy, an expression of the comic vision that Hawkes has said "always suggests futurity . . . always suggests a certain hope in the limitless energies of life itself."[4] If we can take Hawkes at his word, we should view *Second Skin* as a kind of divine comedy, one in which the protagonist, after a life of failure and suffering, earns a peculiar form of redemption.[5] I believe that we should take him at his word and accept *Second Skin*, not simply as a comedy, but as the "romance" that its narrator, Skipper, insists that it is, while recognizing that parody has an important, though subordinate, function in the novel.

I am principally concerned here with the comic structure of *Second*

Skin, most particularly with the double time-scheme that is a major component of its structure. However, since even the time-scheme is partly parodic, some preliminary observations about the function of parody in *Second Skin* seem in order. The pleasures that parody provides us, it is worth remembering, are not exactly the same as those derived from the kind of comedy Hawkes claims to have written. The appeal of parody is almost exclusively intellectual; a reader derives pleasure from recognizing the conventions—of, say, plot, characterization, style, and theme—that the writer parodies and appreciating the cleverness with which he parodies them. A parody is in effect a joke that writer and audience share at the expense of the parodied. It is also a process that calls attention to itself, one in which content is subordinate to technique. In a fictional parody the reader is not encouraged to sympathize with the characters portrayed; they are often themselves objects of parody, sometimes of ridicule. The parodist thus creates a distance between reader and subject that makes sympathy improbable. The purer the parody, the greater the distance. As a result, the pleasures of parody may be sophisticated, but they are not emotionally complicated by sympathy.

The responses that *Second Skin* elicits, on the other hand, are quite complex, because the distance between reader and subject continually varies. The main instrument of Hawkes's parody is Skipper, the narrator and protagonist. He is, by any conventional standard of success, a failure. His "naked history" is that of a weak, sexually incompetent man living in a nightmarish world where physical strength and sexual prowess are the only things that count. During his history he has repeatedly invited and suffered—sometimes, it seems, in a perversely ecstatic way—abuse at the hands of the grotesque characters he has involved himself and his family with. The result has been a series of disasters, including suicide, murder, and sexual degradation, all of them the consequence of his weakness. Yet he insists that we interpret it otherwise:

> High lights of helplessness? Mere trivial record of collapse? Say, rather, that it is the chronicle of recovery, the history of courage, the dead reckoning of my romance, the act of memory, the dance of shadows. And all the earmarks of pageantry, if you will, the glow of Skipper's serpentine tale.[6]

Coming as it does after two chapters that give ample evidence of Skipper's almost embarrassing helplessness, this is bound to strike the reader as plainly absurd, creating a distance between this self-styled singer of the "chronicle of recovery" and his audience.

However, as this passage suggests, Skipper is not simply a narrator providing a "[m]ere trivial record"; he is an artist consciously—and very self-consciously—shaping his "romance." Throughout, he is attentive in the extreme to "plot, character, setting, and theme," never allowing us to forget their significance for him. Clearly, he places great value on those elements of fiction that Hawkes claimed to have abandoned at the outset of his career. Moreover, Skipper has chosen an antiquated literary form (the romance) as the vehicle for a theme (death and rebirth) that has become a cliché of modern fiction. He is a fifty-nine-year-old literary novice who resembles the talented but naive young fiction writer who believes that he is creating something new.[7]

Yet, however naive an artist and unreliable an interpreter of his own history Skipper may be, he is talented, a gifted storyteller with a lyrical tongue and an eye for detail that keep the reader's emotions engaged much of the time. The chapter entitled "Land of Spices," which opens with the passage quoted above, provides a good illustration of the way in which Hawkes creates and then reduces the distance between his narrator and the reader. After telling us what to think of his story, Skipper turns to an episode intended to demonstrate his triumph over the tragic past: the occasion on which he inseminates Sweet Phyllis the cow. In this idyllic "pastoral in [his] time of no time" (p. 166), he gathers his entourage—a group of island women and his old messboy Sonny—and organizes a more or less solemn procession to the grove where the cows are standing. Skipper and his friends enjoy a pastoral banquet, which is followed by a languid siesta, with the characters lying together among the cows in an atmosphere of innocent sensuality. When the time is right, Skipper, acting as artificial inseminator, group leader, and priest, enlists his friends as acolytes in a fertility ritual that reaches its climax when he blows the sperm of Oscar the bull through a pipette into "the windless dark cave" of Sweet Phyllis' womb. Afterwards, there is a single-file recession, and Skipper ends his day with a purifying bath in the ocean.[8]

This episode, an interlude between the most tragic chapters of Skipper's "naked history," is one of the best comic moments of the novel, but the pleasures it gives are not strictly those of parody. To be sure, there is a good deal of parody in the ritualization of the act of artificially inseminating a cow. But Skipper's narration of the episode also elicits a more immediate, sensual response:

So while the spring kept Oscar cool, the five of us sprawled close together and held out our hands to the fat black arm that disappeared inside the pot and came up dripping. Calypso herself couldn't have done better. Sweet guavas and fat meat that slid into the fingers, made the fingers breathe, and crushed leaves of cinnamon on the tongue and sweet shreds of coconut. (p. 168)

The reference to Oscar's sperm is an amusing detail, and the analogy between the huge black woman, Big Bertha, and Calypso keeps the strain of parody alive. But the other details, particularly the references to food and flesh, engage the whole range of the reader's senses, reducing the distance between reader and subject that parody usually creates. The reader comes away from the scene with a double image of the experience—that is, with an image of it as both a parody and a compelling sensual representation of the narrator's subjective experience. And, while there is a parody embedded in it, the episode is nevertheless rendered as convincingly idyllic.

Parody in *Second Skin*, then, seems a part of its total design, but a subordinate part. The novel contains numerous parodies, both formal (rituals like that described above) and incidental (comically inappropriate allusions and excruciating puns like "serpentine tale" and "the golden fleas"), that give shading, texture, and ironic resonance to the bright surface of the narrative. They function in much the same way as parody does in Shakespearean comedy and romance, where it is often the vehicle for expressing anti-romantic ideas that work against but do not discredit the dominant romantic and idealistic impulses in the plays. The allusions to Shakespearean characters, particularly to Ariel and Miranda, suggest that Shakespearean romance may provide a good paradigm for a discussion of *Second Skin*. Skipper's apparent familiarity with *The Tempest* certainly affects his conception of his experience. For instance, the significance of Miranda's name is not lost on him:

I hear that name—Miranda, Miranda!—and once again quicken to its false suggestiveness, feel its rhapsody of sound, the several throbs of the vowels, the very music of charity, innocence, obedience, love. For a moment I seem to see both magic island and imaginary girl. But Miranda was the widow's name—out of what perversity, what improbable desire I am at a loss to say—and no one could have given a more ugly denial to that heartbreaking and softly fluted name than the tall and treacherous woman. (p. 5)

Later, he refers to himself as an "old Ariel in sneakers" (p. 162), but in fact he is a comic version of Prospero. Like Prospero, he is a failed leader whose ineptitude has caused him to be driven from his society to an island, where he attempts to save what is left of his family. Unlike Prospero, however, Skipper fails in his first attempt and is driven to another island, this time alone, where he gains control over his life through the acquisition of a special art—though in his case it is not magic but a skill, the artificial insemination of livestock.

This is obviously parody, and good parody; there is just enough connection between Skipper and Prospero to make an analogy that initially seems ludicrous somehow appropriate. But the relevance of *The Tempest* to *Second Skin* is not strictly a parodic one. Conceptually, Shakespearean romance is entirely compatible with Hawkes's notion that "comic vision always suggests futurity." *The Tempest*, whose action unfolds on a single afternoon, is a play that marks a transition, the laying to rest of a quasi-tragic history (which is narrated at some length by Prospero on a single afternoon) and the start of a bright new future that commences with the betrothal of Ferdinand and Miranda. In both works history is treated, to use Skipper's phrase, as "a dream already dreamt and destroyed" (p. 45), and we are invited to look toward a future in which the aging protagonists, while anticipating their own deaths, are happy in the confidence that they have contributed to the renewal of life.[9] In Shakespeare's play this is accomplished by relegating tragic history to narrative while rendering Prospero's control of events and people in dramatic form. In *Second Skin* it is accomplished by Skipper's narrative technique, which involves the employment of a double time-scheme.

Skipper has contrived his romance of death and rebirth by juxtaposing two narratives: his "naked history," which is a chronicle of death, and his "diary of the artificial inseminator," which culminates in the birth of Catalina Kate's baby. He frames these narratives with a prologue and epilogue; in the first chapter he invokes his "muses," the ghosts from his past; in the last, he and his friends celebrate the birth of Kate's baby in a cemetery. Thus the prologue is a kind of exhumation of the dead, while the epilogue is a symbolic reburial of them in the context of the celebration of a redemptive birth.

In outline, Skipper's manipulation of the themes of death and rebirth is quite mechanical, a fact which by itself causes us to suspect that Hawkes is parodying a thematic and structural convention that Skipper treats with utter seriousness. There is also a suggestion of parody in the mystery surrounding the conception of Kate's baby, about which Skipper is elusive. Is the baby Skipper's or Sonny's? Is it the product of natural or artificial insemination? Skipper and Sonny bask in sensuality on the wandering island, and at one point Skipper, in a characteristically ambiguous way, implies that he has recovered his sexual potency there:

> Now I have Catalina Kate. . . . And this—Sonny and I both agree—this is love. Here I have only to drop my trousers—no shirt, no undershirt, no shorts—to awaken paradise itself, awaken it with the sympathetic sound of Catalina Kate's soft laughter. (p. 46)

But Skipper keeps returning to his triumph as artificial inseminator, directly linking all of his accomplishments on the island to the acquisition of his new art. The birth of Kate's child is to be his crowning accomplishment:

> So in six months and on the Night of All Saints Catalina Kate will bear her child—our child—and I shall complete my history, my evocation through a golden glass, my hymn to the invisible changing serpents of the wind, complete this the confession of my triumph, this my diary of an artificial inseminator. (p. 49)

The baby, ambiguously referred to as "our child," proves to be "three times as black" (p. 209) as Catalina Kate, who denies that it looks like either Skipper or Sonny. Thus the mystery is sustained, teasing us with the suggestion that what we have here is a broad parody of the Immaculate Conception (accomplished, perhaps through artificial insemination) and the Nativity.

Skipper juxtaposes the two narratives that make up the body of the novel in a way that calls attention to the death and rebirth themes. The prologue, epilogue, and diary chapters, in which the dominant tense is the present, establish the temporal level which is the telling of the story itself. This is appropriate, for life on the wandering island, in Skipper's "time of no time," is not an historical sequence but a timeless process of renewal without historical identity. Skipper's awareness of this process gives him the basis for constructing his novel. He himself is on the threshold of old age; his fifty-ninth birthday coincides with the birth of Kate's baby on All Saints Day. But the birth, the anticipation that Kate will conceive again in a few weeks, and the continuing calls of the cows to be inseminated confirm the process of renewal—and Skipper's belief in his immortality.

It is this belief that has allowed Skipper, after seven years on the wandering island, to confront his history, subdue his enemies, and turn his failures into triumphs through art. His art is itself synchronized to the life process, specifically to Kate's pregnancy. From the clues that Skipper provides in the present-tense chapters, it is clear that his narration takes him just over nine months; the prologue is written on the eve of Kate's conception, the epilogue on the night following the baby's baptism. Also, there is a nearly perfect month-by-month correspondence between the progress of Kate's pregnancy and the structure of Skipper's narrative of events that took place before he entered his "time of no time" on the island. Chapters two and three are devoted to the history; in chapter four, Skipper turns to his diary, noting that Kate is three months pregnant. In chapters five and six, he returns to the history. Chapter seven is another diary chapter, in which Skipper announces that Kate is now six months pregnant. Thus, to this point it is clear that each of the six chapters, two through seven, corresponds to a month of Kate's term. There is a break in the pattern, however, in chapters eight and nine, which apparently take Skipper only a month to write, for he mentions in chapter ten that Kate still has four weeks to go. In these last four weeks Skipper writes the climactic chapter of the history, which culminates in Cassandra's suicide. This event, the structure suggests, coincides with the birth of Kate's baby in the narrative present.

By compressing his history and rearranging its events, Skipper also succeeds in relating the history to Kate's pregnancy in a symbolic way. His narration of the history begins *in media res*, at the point where he is about to move what is left of his family from the west coast to a "black island" in the north Atlantic. His life is already a history of failure—as a son, husband, father and naval officer—and this move is a last attempt to redeem himself by preserving the life of his suicidal daughter Cassandra. But Skipper's effort is clearly doomed from the start. Ominously, Cassandra makes him submit to the "vulgar art" of the tattooer, who letters the name of her homosexual ex-husband on Skipper's breast, an action that foreshadows the humiliations that Skipper is to endure on the black island. And Cassandra's responsiveness to the lurid kisses of a group of AWOL soldiers who accost her on the southwestern desert anticipates her fatal involvement in sexual intrigue later. Skipper's narration of this futile "journey to the East" coincides with the first two months of Kate's pregnancy, the opening phase of the symbolic journey of the embryo to maturity. Later, he will place the climaxes of these journeys—one ending in suicide and abortion, the other in birth—in obviously contrasting juxtaposition.

Skipper narrates chapters five and six, which describe the fall and winter months on the north Atlantic island, during the middle months, or "winter," of Kate's pregnancy. These chapters are dominated by the sinister Miranda, the black widow. Miranda, dark and voluptuous, is an obvious contrast to the frail, blonde Cassandra, but the two women are really complementary figures, since both are associated with death. Where Cassandra is suicidal, Miranda glories in an aggressive, destructive sexuality while rejecting the creative side of sexual experience. One of her first acts after Skipper, Cassandra, and the infant Pixie move into her house is to cut the nipples off Pixie's baby bottles. And later, in the aftermath of Cassandra's suicide, she giftwraps the girl's aborted fetus as a macabre joke on Skipper. During the intervening months she has become Skipper's rival by appointing herself surrogate mother (she even makes Cassandra a dress to wear to a high school dance), all the while luring Cassandra away from Skipper's influence and into sexual involvement with the lecherous Captain Red and Jomo.

Both Cassandra and Miranda are contrasted to Catalina Kate, whose character becomes defined in chapter seven. There, Skipper tells of finding Kate lying at the edge of a swamp with her belly in a hole in the sand. There is an iguana on her back. The animal, in the attitude of a male fertilizing a female ("His head reached her shoulders, his tail dropped over her buttocks" [p. 105]), has dug its claws into her flesh. Skipper attempts to pull the iguana off, but the animal only clutches more tightly, and he is obliged to give up. In spite of the obvious pain this causes, Kate remains perfectly still, and after several hours the animal crawls away. Here, the stoical Kate is a sharp contrast to the destructive Miranda and suicidal Cassandra—in fact, to all "the sand-scratchers, the impatient sufferers of self-inflicted death" (p. 2) who populate Skipper's history. Her submission to the iguana, as she rehearses for the coming birth by imitating the reptile who lays and buries its eggs in the sand, suggests an acceptance of the primitive idea that animals are the distant progenitors of humans, that (in this case) the iguana is an ancestor of the baby and has a share in its paternity. She thus instinctively acknowledges the unbroken connection between past and present, and, as one about to give birth to the future, she epitomizes the unity of all parts of time which Skipper finds on this island.

As Kate enters the final phase of her pregnancy, Skipper accelerates his narration of the history, taking just one month for chapters eight and nine. In this section he abandons chronological order, relating episodes thematically. Chapter eight is a short history of domestic failure in which Skipper tells of Cassandra's ludicrous and ill-fated marriage to Fernandez (a fiasco for which Skipper is held responsible) and of the death of his wife, Gertrude, who responded to Skipper's impotence through alcholism, adultery, and suicide. This chapter is a prelude to "The Brutal Act," in which Skipper turns to the most violent and tragic incidents in his life. He recounts the *Starfish* mutiny, at the height of which he was sexually assaulted by his "devil," Tremlow. He tells of finding, during his last shore patrol in New York, the body of Fernandez, murdered during a homosexual encounter. All of these events are linked by the central fact of Skipper's impotence, and his narration of them amounts to a confession. Appropriately, he concludes chapter nine by relating his father's suicide, the incident which was the germ of all of Skipper's failures because it robbed him of a model for his masculine identity.

In chapter ten, Skipper interrupts his history to tell of the idyllic interlude discussed earlier. This chapter differs radically in mood and movement from those that surround it. It is, as I have pointed out, essentially comic, and the languid, sensual movement of the characters is contrasted to the accelerating violence of the adjacent chapters of the history. Here, Skipper, always a victim in his former life, completely controls events, even the pace of human movement. And his successful insemination of Sweet Phyllis foreshadows the birth of Kate's baby, in which he finds his redemption from the failures he is chronicling. This interlude functions, then, to anticipate the comic resolution and to establish in the reader a balanced perspective on the tragic events of the history; it reminds us that Skipper's romance is after all "the chronicle of recovery," and this makes the devastating violence of the history supportable.

The narrative picks up speed again in chapter eleven, where Skipper tells of Cassandra's seduction on the *Peter Poor* and of the wild hot rod chase that ends with his discovery of her suicide. The accelerating pace of this chapter reflects, I think, both Skipper's eagerness of having done with his naked history and his anticipation of the redemptive birth, to which he has synchronized the history. The climax of the history occurs very near the end of this chapter, which suggests that Skipper has timed his narration so that Cassandra's abortion-suicide coincides with Kate's delivery.

In the brief denouement that follows Cassandra's death, Skipper endures one last humiliation by Miranda, who presents him with the giftwrapped fetus. Just before he leaves the island for good, Skipper buries the unopened package in Cassandra's grave. The juxtaposition of these events with the birth and baptism of Kate's baby provides a central symbolic contrast between Skipper's lives in two worlds. At the conclusion of his history Cassandra, the suicidal anti-mother, and Miranda, her morbid midwife, have presented Skipper with a dead fetus, symbol of the blight that infects the world of the naked history. On the other side, Kate, the primitive earth-mother, has presented him with a healthy child, symbolizing the perpetual renewal in his paradisical new world. The presentations are both acknowledged in graveyard rituals, but there is an important difference between them: the ritual on the black island is simply a burial; that on the wandering island is a celebration of renewal and, in fact, a denial of the finality of death. For when Skipper asks Kate who the baby looks like, she answers that he looks "like the fella in the grave" (p. 209) at which they conduct their ceremony, indicating that the dead are resurrected in the newly born.

Again, in outline this structure seems quite mechanical. But Skipper's art is far from crude, and it is only when we reduce the novel to a structural outline that we become aware of his deliberate juxtaposition of plots and themes. For Skipper links his two narratives with a wealth of images and motifs, and the "bright needlepoint" of his art creates, as one critic puts it, "a garment of real beauty."[10] A thorough discussion of the interrelationship of incidents, images, and motifs, and their contribution to the total coherence of *Second Skin*, might well run as long as the novel itself. I would like to discuss briefly two of the prominent motifs that reinforce Skipper's double time-scheme: the wind, to which his heart and skin "have always been especially sensitive" (p. 3), and the contrasting forms of locomotion emphasized in the two narratives.

In the present-tense chapters Skipper repeatedly alludes to the "serpentine wind" that envelops the wandering island:

> But the wind, this bundle of invisible snakes, roars across our wandering
> island—it *is* a wandering island, of course, unlocated in space and quite out
> of time—and seems to heap the shoulders with an armlike weight, to coil
> about my naked legs and pulse and cool and caress the flesh with an

unpredictable weight and consistency, tension, of its own. These snakes that fly in the wind are as large around as tree trunks; but pliant, as ever-lasting pliant, as the serpents that crowd my dreams. So the wind nests it-self and bundles itself across this island, buffets the body with wedges of in-visible but still sensual configurations. (p. 46)

This wind is contrasted to the hot wind that blew across the southwest-ern desert in chapter two and "made a rasping noise of all the debris of the desert: tiny cellular spines, dead beetles, the discarded translucent tissue of wandering snakes, the offal of embryonic lizards and fields of dead dry locusts" (p. 35). It is contrasted even more sharply to the "black wind . . . rising off the iron flanks of the Atlantic" (p. 53) that destroys life on the black island, gradually reducing it to a rocky skele-ton. The serpentine wind, "hotter and colder, and more persistent, more soft or more strong and indecent, in its touch" (p. 46) than the other winds, is essentially benevolent, and where those punishing winds continue to erode the waste lands of history, the serpentine wind pushes the wandering island through Skipper's "time of no time," ensuring the perpetual renewal of life.

The serpent is a central metaphor of Skipper's new life, as he analo-gizes "this bundle of invisible snakes" with "the serpents that crowd [his] dreams" and his "serpentine tale." It is a highly appropriate one, for in the iconography of ancient pagan mythologies the serpent often appeared as a symbol of rebirth—an association that derives, probably, from the ability of the snake to moult, to renew its life by shedding its old skin. The title of the novel is tantalizing; one is tempted to look for (and he can easily find) "second skins" everywhere—not only in the oil-skins that Skipper explicitly identifies as his second skin (p. 180), but in the uniforms that he puts on and off, in the changes in the condition of his natural skin, even in his changes of role. If we take the serpent to be the central image in the novel, all of these associations are valid, for in the snake the process of moulting is recurrent: as soon as he sheds his old skin he begins to outgrow the new one, and so must eventually moult that. So it is with Skipper, who in his lifetime "outgrows"—-ironically, because he has failed in them—his assumed roles as son, husband, father, officer. And in moments of crisis he is either forced to shed or change clothes or becomes aware that his clothes are too tight. Thus his clothes are ripped from him during the *Starfish* mutiny; he is confined in ill-fitting oilskins on the *Peter Poor*; he finds that the web belt and gaiters he wears on his last shore patrol, when he discovers the murdered Fernandez, are uncomfortably tight. Significantly, Skipper's "uniform" on the wandering island consists only of the more comfortable and durable remnants of his naval uniform and his own skin, which the sun and serpentine wind have so darkened that his mark of shame, the tattoo on his breast, is nearly invisible.

The motif that best demonstrates the difference between the new Skipper and the old, between the failed naval officer and "the AI" who is the acknowledged leader of his little society, is perhaps that of locomotion. In the history, movement from one place to another is often rapid, violent, and machine-driven. The characters, most of whom are bent on destruction, travel to disaster in vehicles that are associated with the agents of death, violence, and sexual depravity in the novel. The hearse is associated with Skipper's mortician father, hotrods with Miranda and Jomo, the *Peter Poor* with Captain Red, and the *Starfish* with Tremlow. Skipper even feels threatened by the Greyhound bus—driven, he observes, by a "mean nigger" (p. 26)—that takes him and his family east and by the silhouette of a ship, "ugly span of pointed iron" (p. 4), that he sees on the horizon off the wandering island. Throughout the history Skipper conventionally equates machines with male sexuality, regarding those associated with them as threats to his own ambiguous manhood.

These machines are also emblems of the nightmare world of the mid-twentieth century, a world in which Skipper cannot function well. He is fat, slow, and irresolute, and his actions are always out of synchrony with events. He repeatedly arrives at the scene of a disaster too late to prevent its occurrence; he can only be witness to the bloody aftermath of tragedies like the deaths of Gertrude, Fernandez, and Cassandra. At other times, his lack of resolve makes him ineffectual; he temporizes with threatening characters and situations until it is too late to prevent the threats from becoming actualities. His indecision allows the *Starfish* mutiny to get out of hand, and he spends an entire winter wishfully appealing to the best instincts of Miranda and her friends as they pull Cassandra away from him and toward her death. Physically and psychologically, Skipper lags behind everyone else, with the result that he is never able to redeem himself by preventing the destruction of those he claims to care about.

On the wandering island, however, Skipper is able to synchronize the movement of events with his own actions, and, as artificial inseminator, he can even exercise some control over the processes of life itself. He has gained this control partly because he is no longer threatened by sexually aggressive males or their machines. The only convincing embodiment of male sexual energy on the island is, comically, Oscar the bull, and Skipper keeps him penned up. The only form of locomotion here is the natural one of walking, at which Skipper professes to excel:

> As a walker, for instance, I am a tiger. I have always walked far in my white socks, my white shoes, and the extent and manner of my walking have always been remarked upon, with admiration or maliciousness, in the past. . . . Of course there are those who laugh. But others, like Sonny, recognize my need, my purpose, my strength and grace. Always my strength and grace. (p. 3)

The need and purpose alluded to here seem to be, respectively, leadership and nurture. Throughout the novel, leadership and the esteem, so often denied him in his naked history, accorded to an acknowledged leader are major preoccupations of Skipper's. Significantly, when he goes to inseminate Sweet Phyllis he makes the short journey to the grove a procession that confirms his role as leader:

> To the last we held our single file. To the last we maintained our evenly spaced formation, our gentle steps, delicate order, significant line. . . . Sniffing the sweet air and keeping my chin lifted, and swaying, riding slowly forward at a heavy contented angle I, Skipper, led the way. I knew the way, was the man in charge—the AI—and there was no mistaking me for anything but the leader now, and they were my faithful followers, my entourage. (p. 166)

Walking, the only form of locomotion over which one has complete control, allows Skipper to preserve the "delicate order" and "significant line" that the chaotic, headlong motion of the machines in his naked history obliterated.

The ultimate purpose served by Skipper's control is nurture, the preservation and cultivation of life. For him the art of the artificial inseminator is an exalted and redemptive one that has freed him from the legacy of guilt and death left him by his mortician father:

> And the work itself? Artificial Insemination. Cows. In my flapping tennis shoes and naval cap and long puffy sun-bleached trousers, and accompanied by my assistant, Sonny, I am much esteemed as the man who inseminates the cows and causes these enormous soft animals to bring forth calves. . . . The mere lowing of a herd, you see, has become my triumph. Yes, my tri-

umph now. And how different from my morbid father's. And haven't I re-
deemed his profession, his occupation, with my own? I think so. (p. 47)

The insemination of these cows has given Skipper the satisfaction of
private retaliation against his old enemies—"Miranda will never know
how many slick frisky calves have been conceived in her name" (p.
48)—but the "best evidence" of his triumph, he says, is Catalina Kate,
whose pregnancy has allowed Skipper to resurrect his history and "to
recount even the smallest buried detail of [his] life with Miranda" (p.
48) and the other figures who have haunted him.

Earlier, I mentioned the mystery surrounding the conception of
Kate's child. Whatever Skipper's role in that has been, the birth cycle
is part of his conscious design, for he has used it as a means of
subordinating the episodes of a tragic and chaotic history to his ultimate purpose of celebrating his own redemption. In him the artificial
inseminator and writer of romance merge in a reciprocity between
Skipper's practical and literary arts. His involvement in the process of
birth has both enabled him to face his past and provided him with a
structure for reordering it in a satisfying way. He has achieved, in his
own mind at least, a nearly ideal condition in which man harmonizes
the practical with the imaginative, unifying life and art.

At the end of the novel Skipper sees himself as passing out of his
"time of no time" into a state of timelessness:

> And now? Now I sit at my long table in the middle of my loud wandering
> night and by the light of a candle . . . I watch this final flourish of my own
> hand and muse and blow away the ashes and listen to the breathing among
> the rubbery leaves and the insects sweating out the night. Because now I am
> fifty-nine years old and I knew I would be, and now there is the sun in the
> evening, the moon at dawn, the still voice. That's it. The sun in the even-
> ing. The moon at dawn. The still voice. (p. 210)

Like Prospero, Skipper, his work finally done, closes the book. His
seven years on the island, during which he has learned that "history is a
dream already dreamt and destroyed," have prepared him for this last
transition. The island itself has provided this lesson, for it has survived
repeated invasions from the historical world. The decayed plantation
house in which Skipper lives, the broken water-wheel he identifies as a
"Monolith of forgotten industry" (p. 103), and the mauve habit of a
vanished sisterhood that Sister Josie wears are all evidence of some futile effort to make the island a part of history, fixing it in place and

time. Yet the island remains in a natural evolutionary state: home of the iguana, the wild cows, the primitive natives, and, of course, Skipper and Sonny. It thus contains both past and present, having absorbed the transitory historical in its timelessness. In this respect it serves as a metaphor of Skipper's evolving relationship with his own history; like the island, Skipper has absorbed history and destroyed it.

The double-time scheme in *Second Skin*, like that of Shakespearean romance, has enabled Skipper to make this claim convincingly. By compressing the fifty-odd years of his earlier life and confining it within the framework of the nine-month cycle of Catalina Kate's pregnancy, Skipper has managed to subordinate the notion of time as the agent of destruction to that of time as the agent of renewal in a restorative pattern. Life becomes, not a series of finite events (which in Skipper's case have been tragic), but a process of *becoming* which is not finite: the baby eventually becomes "the fella in the grave" who is resurrected, in a sense, in the baby. In his particular life Skipper, the impotent failure of the naked history, has become the creator of both life and art, bringing his twin efforts, the baby and the book, to completion at once. His voice becomes still, presumably, because it is time for him to become something else.

NOTES

1. "John Hawkes: An Interview," *Wisconsin Studies in Contemporary Literature*, 6 (1965), 149.

2. Ibid., p. 149.

3. Norman F. Laver, in "The Structure of *Second Skin*," *Novel*, 5 (1972), 208–14, discusses the novel's structure wholly in terms of parody. While he makes a number of interesting and useful comparisons between *Second Skin* and the traditional American novel (as described by Richard Chase), the Arcadian romance, and *The Golden Ass*, his discussion is misleading in its neglect of the larger comic purposes of the novel.

4. "John Hawkes: An Interview," p. 146.

5. Since that time Hawkes has recanted some of his earlier statements about fiction. In a colloquy with John Barth ("Hawkes and Barth Talk about Fiction," *New York Times Book Review*, April 1, 1979), he admitted that his denunciation of "plot, setting, theme, and character" was inspired by the fact "that these terms lent themselves to use by pedantic and dull teachers of literature" (p. 31). He acknowledged the necessity for plot, though claiming not to know what plot is. He also indicated that, since writing *Second Skin* he has abandoned comedy as "too comforting" (p. 31).

6. *Second Skin* (New York: New Directions, 1963), p. 162. Future page references will be made parenthetically in the text.

7. It is tempting to suspect that Hawkes, in using Skipper thus, was animated by a motive not uncommon to the parodist: the desire to indulge oneself while excusing oneself. By having Skipper write the romance of death and rebirth, Hawkes was able to construct, quite unabashedly, the kind of Great Novel that a writer of his sophistication would not allow himself to attempt.

8. In the Wisconsin interview Hawkes provided an interesting sidelight to Skipper's purifying bath: the writer himself went through the same ritual every afternoon on the West Indies island on which he wrote *Second Skin*—in order, he said, "to wash away the filth of creative effort" (p. 146).

9. At the conclusion of *The Tempest*, Prospero announces his intention to retire in Milan, "where / Every third thought shall be [his] grave" (V.1.310–11).

10. Tony Tanner, *City of Words: American Fiction, 1950–1970* (London: Jonathan Cape, 1971), p. 229.

Reestablishing Innocence:
A Conversation with Leslie A. Fiedler

Geoffrey Green
University of Southern California

GREEN: I would like this conversation to encompass both aspects of your artistic sensibility: the literary-cultural critic and the creator of fiction. And I would like to begin by exploiting that unique dual perspective in order to touch upon your feelings concerning the state of contemporary fiction as well as your notion of yourself as a fiction writer within that literary environment.

FIEDLER: I have this funny double feeling about the way things are right now as far as writers of fiction are concerned. It's a time of absolute open possibilities, on the one hand: this is a time when, in a way, it's possible for a writer of fiction to do almost anything because though various groups who talk to each other think that there are certain fictional modes which are dominant, that, in fact, is not true. There never was a time when more different kinds of fiction were being written. But the same thing which makes the situation an open situation makes it a very difficult situation: where everything is permitted, nobody really knows what he wants to do.

G: I'd like to look back now at an essay you wrote almost twenty years ago, "An Almost Imaginary Interview: Hemingway in Ketchum." In that piece, you posit a fictional macho Hemingway, a myth of cultural fabrication, in opposition to a supposedly actual insecure and feeble Hemingway with whom the essayist-narrator is holding a frustrating conversation; then you suggest that Hemingway is experiencing a similar polarity between the Leslie Fiedler he has fabricated as a reductive critic and the actual complex person before him: then you state, "the critic is obliged only to the truth though he knows that truth is never completely in his grasp." Does that still strike you as an exemplary statement about your work?

F: Yes, it does. And it suggests another thing which I don't know whether I said in the essay but it's sure what your quoting it back to me stirs in my mind: it seems to me maybe, in retrospect, that I was more the victim of a similar kind of conflict between my two selves than I was willing to admit or capable of knowing at the time. The critic, just like the writer of fiction, after a while creates a fictional self who tends to take over his own writing from him; after you've written your first critical work, you're in exactly the same sort of plight as the novelist or the short story writer is after he's written his first thing. He becomes the victim of the first fiction which he creates of himself—as a critic, as a novelist, as a short story writer. All my life, I keep fighting to get back to find my own full, natural human voice so that I can be responding to those books as whatever that indefinable thing is that I really am instead of the Leslie Fiedler which I've already created in my earlier work.

G: Your position reminds me of a story which you must have read after you wrote the essay, Borges's "Theme of the Traitor and the Hero"; it deals with the parallel imaginative dreams that writers fabricate to incorporate each other within their subjective realms.

F: Borges is always saying things which, for me, seem like dreams I've had or thoughts that have passed through my head—that's one of the reasons I like to read him, but you get into an infinite regress that way. Ceasing to be Leslie Fiedler the critic responding to literature, I then become Leslie Fiedler the man who is trying not to be the critic responding to literature but to be the whole Leslie Fiedler again . . . this sounds more and more Borgesian, doesn't it, as it goes on?

G: I guess you're saying that there are limits to subjectivity just as there are limits to objectivity .

F: The "I" is something that you invent just like the "he"s and the "she"s and the "you"s that you're talking about.

G: Are you suggesting that if you carry subjectivity to its limits, it can become ultimately facetious?

F: That myth of oneself that one creates is just as real as anything else, so he might as well speak from wherever he is at the moment. What you have to constantly do is subvert and transcend that already-created self. I have this dream of that endlessly-retreating subjectivity which

I'm trying to find. I committed myself long, long ago—in reaction to the conventions in which I grew up—to the personal voice, rather than the impersonal voice. I decided that I was going to be an "I" critic instead of a voice *ex cathedra*. I know—just the way the writer of fiction knows—that the "I" of the critic is a fiction, too.

G: It seems to me that you have always been striving to enunciate the reality that lurks beneath the superficial appearance of things, but then at the same time, affirming the difficulty of ever attaining that truth absolutely.

F: That's right. One of the terms I've always used for myself as a critic is that I'm a cryptanalytic critic: I take every text as being primarily interesting for its encoded meanings, rather than its apparent meanings. I'm always trying to break that code, but how can you ever tell?

G: Until subsequent events reveal it in a different sense.

F: Right, and then you think: maybe I was right enough then, now it's time to be more right or right in a different direction.

G: A mere sampling of the titles of your books—*Love and Death in the American Novel*; *An End to Innocence*; *No! In Thunder*; *Pull Down Vanity*; *Waiting for the End*; *To the Gentiles*—would suggest a concern with polarity, with the process of opposition within the cultural imagination.

F: Yes, I guess I'm interested in polarities, but when I look at my titles, what they always suggest to me is that I'm very fond of words like *death* of the novel, or an *end* to innocence: it's as if I feel better when I look back than when I look forward. Sometimes I project myself into the future in order to look back on the present, but I'm always assuming that I'm looking at the end of something and speculating about new beginnings. But I've been haunted by that *end*. . . . The other thing in which I'm very obviously interested is the whole question of innocence: I'm always talking about innocence ending, but that's just my own way of rediscovering a new kind of innocence. I would love to be an innocent kind of "I" looking at literature.

G: Isn't that kind of "I" ironic in that it presupposes an innocence compromised in the process of attempting to regain itself?

F: I think of it as the reverse of that: one doesn't know what innocence is until he knows he's compromised. If you can say to yourself, "I'm compromised," then you have some notion of what it was that you lost or bartered away. I'm not interested in the innocence of a child because it doesn't exist; you only know what innocence is when you're able to say, "I was innocent and I'm no longer innocent; I would like to recover innocence," or "I'm embarrassed by innocence."

G: Where does that innocence that you're attracted to come from? What does it emanate from?

F: I don't know. I'm puzzled about it all the time. It's interesting that the first longish story I ever published was called "The Fear of Innocence," and the first book of essays I ever published was called *An End to Innocence.*

G: Would you say that innocence is a state, or a feeling, or a kind of intuition?

F: I think innocence is a state but you only know it when you're expelled from it. Adam didn't know he was in the Garden until he was outside the Garden. It was only then that he said, "I've been thrown out of the Garden." The Garden is the place you've been kicked out of.

G: It's a nice metaphor for a detached critical process.

F: Yes, I hope so.

G: It suggests that process of rereading which orders all information.

F: In an effort to find out what there was there to be ordered to begin with: I guess that's what innocence means to me. It's the original chaos, the unorganized, the intuitive, the impulsive.

G: The subtitle of this volume is "Novel vs. Fiction." When you made your controversial statement some years ago that the novel is dead, were you conceiving of fiction and the novel in this sort of conceptual opposition so that you could affirm the novel's end as opposed to the continuing viability of fiction?

F: The word "fiction" is not a word that is important to me; my word is "story." "Story" is unending. I suppose, if we want to stay with this metaphor that we started with—innocent narrative I call *story* . . . unreflexive narrative. The novel I think of as a particular form which began at a certain historical moment and which will cease to be viable at another moment. I think there is a hangover of Marxism in my notion of the novel: I think of the novel as a form which belongs to the dominance of the bourgeoisie. With the loss of nerve on the part of the bourgeoisie, the novel ceases to be the dominant form, or it threatens to cease to be the dominant form, or at least, it becomes problematic. In the days of Richardson, the novel wasn't problematic—it was just what you did; it was the form which you thought of as being out there for fiction. I suppose in the days when the novel was being invented that there was even an illusion in people's heads that this was going to be the supreme form of narrative. All the things which had tentatively been done and failed—romances and so forth—were suddenly going to have a coherence and order which would be superior to anything that came before and afterwards; there could be only decline.

G: Are you suggesting that—by grounding the literary form within this kind of social context—when forms do change and evolve, there is a parallel change in the consciousness and mores of the people who read them?

F: Yes, I would assume that first, certain objective conditions change. Then consciousness and sensibility change. And then the literary forms change.

G: In your recent *Salmagundi* essay, "The Death and Rebirths of the Novel," you proclaim that the novel is "dead as a single genre—*the* single genre capable of unifying a society otherwise divided by ideology and taste between male and female, young and old, white and non-white, educated and uneducated, sophisticated and naive."

F: I think in some ways that narrative in film does that better now than the novel does.

G: But how could any one generic form ever hope to reconcile such antithetical oppositions?

F: It only does so insofar as its basic content remains unconscious. The novel did this before it became too self-conscious as a form. After the novel had become hyper-conscious and reflexive, film in some ways was still unfallen, or innocent, and therefore it could unite people. The point—which I've made over and over again in things that I write—is that where we're most conscious, we're most divided—in terms of allegiances, loyalties, party platforms, commitments to programs of action. The place where we're still all together, whatever else divides us, is in the deep imagination. Free storytelling has its roots in that kind of archetypal unconscious. When it loses that, when novels begin to use myth in a secondary way, like Joyce, let's say, then instead of creating a story which is absolutely polysemous, multivalent (it can't be pinned down to a single meaning), it gets to be, in fact, myth interpretation—the myth of Ulysses, says Joyce, means thus and so, and isn't it interesting that it turns out to be like the myth of Hamlet, and so forth: then we're in a place where he excludes certain people from responding.

G: Are you suggesting that as Joyce makes almost anthropological comments upon the subject of the myth that he is moving away from pure, or innocent, storytelling?

F: Right. He's beginning to allegorize or euhemerize.

G: What, then, constitutes the art of pure storytelling?

F: You can see it in two ways. Joyce seems to me a marvelous example—the whole *Ulysses*, in particular. There is Stephen Dedalus's part of *Ulysses*; and that part exists on the level of consciousness, it exists on the level of interpretation, the exclusivist and excluding. And then suddenly, Joyce, without quite knowing what he's doing, invents a character who exists as a kind of free myth, Bloom, and the meanings of Bloom, since they're out of his control, have the kind of universal appeal that one doesn't get when Stephen is explaining Shakespeare, for example.

G: So there's a power which accompanies the bringing of innocence to consciousness?

F: It's what happens when he—instead of bringing everything to the analytical level—allows himself to be submerged in the flow of his own unconscious, his own reveries and nightmares. Joyce freely invents a trail which will somehow accommodate this.

G: Isn't Joyce attempting to order his unconscious materials?

F: He sure is, but my point is that there is a place where the novel passes out of his control and that's when it gets really interesting. Next to Melville, Joyce is the most self-conscious writer that ever existed; but he's also like Melville in another way: he has such total access to the lower levels of his own consciousness that stuff comes up which even he can't control.

G: In "The Death and Rebirths of the Novel," you state that "the invention of the categories of pop and high art were harmful in the beginning, and have by now become totally unviable." Is all literary history, then, a movement toward the creation of demarcational categories and differentiations followed by an innate sloughing off of these intellectual classifications?

F: Those categories which become so harmful: as long as they belonged just to the critics, they didn't work against literature—as long as they were *post facto*. It was only afterwards, looking back, starting at the end of the nineteenth century, that critics decided, say, that Wells belonged mostly on the popular side, James belonged on the side of elite or a high literature, but when James and Wells were writing back and forth to each other and asking each other advice about their stories, they weren't conscious of these distinctions. The strange thing (which was beginning to happen then but really didn't get bad until the rise of high modernism in the early part of the twentieth century) was that the critical categories—categories which had been established *post facto*—entered into the consciousness of the writers so that *before the fact* they were already beginning to write to be classified as high literature, or pop—and that's when you're in trouble.

G: Wasn't a writer like Joyce, for instance, aware of this situation?

F: He sure was: Joyce was one of the great culprits in this whole thing. The fortunate part of Joyce is that he was nutty enough to pass out of his own control. I think that when Joyce is the victim of his own theorizing, then he is really in bad trouble. This was especially true for Joyce toward the end of his life, when he had this whole circle around him who kept telling him what he was doing, that he was really making a revolution of words, and so forth. When a writer writes, sometimes it blessedly happens to him that he can write innocent fiction again. Another favorite example of mine is Nabokov, in *Lolita*.

G: Aren't you equating contrivance with consciousness?

F: A writer has to contrive: there's no other way—you have to figure out what syntax is and how to get from one place to another; as soon as you begin thinking about transitions or even some simple questions like where you end a chapter or where you start your book or what the last sentence is, you're contriving, in a way. Really naive story is sort of a seamless web—there are no beginnings and ends to the story.

G: In these two examples of *Ulysses* and *Lolita*, are you saying that in spite of the attempts of the authors to elaborately order their materials, an innate or unconscious energy or vitality emerged which was larger than the author's efforts to enclose it?

F: Right. You could say, if you liked, that the characters took over: Lolita took over from Nabokov, Bloom took over from Joyce; or you could say just that the material took over. A writer's prayer ought to be that he goes blessedly out of control.

G: It's interesting that a popular writer such as Jacqueline Susann during her frequent appearances on the Tonight Show used to claim that her characters wrote her book, but a literary writer such as John Hawkes prides himself on being detached, on having complete control over his characters and materials.

F: There are some writers who we put in the category of high fiction whose characters take over—Faulkner would be an example. Faulkner, years after he's written a book, can tell you what the characters have been doing since—which a formalist critic would tell you is nonsense. Or Balzac,—who is on that middle line between high and popular, and who thought of his characters as existing independently of his own will: I'm absolutely convinced that one of the gifts of a great writer of fiction is the gift of being possessed by hallucinations which he then, if he is skillful enough, can translate in such a way that you accept them as your own hallucinations.

G: To what extent is our critical appreciation of stories and their forms based upon other than conscious impulses and resources?

F: There is an innocent way of reading: when one is young and he is first beginning to read, what he does is to allow the stories to possess him. As soon as you develop an interest in possessing the story rather than letting the story possess you, then you fall into what gets the critic into trouble. There are very few critics who have ever been able to say intelligent things about books without betraying their own reactions. Lawrence could do it as a critic. Nietzsche could do it; he would be another one: *The Birth of Tragedy* seems to be one of those books. Charles Olson did it, in his Melville book.

G: Are you referring to a quality of subservience to the book?

F: I take quite seriously the metaphor I began with: it's a question of letting the book possess you—the most simple-minded kind of reader lets the book possess him, flipping the pages faster and faster, as quick as he can, hating it when the dream is over. I don't mean a critic doesn't have a right to go back and say, "Jesus, you know how he really did it: when it comes to the most crucial part of the book, instead of rendering the scene, he skips it and lets it be picked up in retrospect later." You can admire the ingenuity and the craftsmanship, but unless there's a kind of surrender—which I don't think of as being humble, exactly . . . you know, I hate really humble criticism.

G: Might we think of it as holding back one's own critical expectations to the way of the text?

F: Sometimes great things happen when you pick up a text, against all your own preconceptions: it's the kind of book you don't like, it's got a point of view which you hate: I think of Dr. Johnson reading Milton, for instance, and getting overwhelmed by him, all the same.

G: If story is pure and remains as a constant possibility within everyone's imagination, how do you account for the periodic embrace and then rejection of such trends as storytelling-for-its-own-sake, narrative, artifice, self-reflexivity, emphasis on theme, etc., throughout fictional works of the last hundred years?

F: There are various reasons for it. Sometimes the motivation behind the distracted story is pretty ignoble; it's kind of snobbist. When it comes to telling a story, scrupulosity in writing doesn't finally count, careful preparation doesn't count, it seems to be a gift. And some pretty *schlubby* characters have been great storytellers. And so I think there has been a tendency in recent years (but it's happened off and on all through the history of the writing of fiction) for some writers to emphasize the things which distinguish the gifted or the diligent person from another. Besides snobbism, there is a kind of covert Protestant ethic which sometimes enters into the situation. The only thing that's worthwhile is the stuff that requires hard work: if you sit all day like Flaubert rewriting one sentence until you get it absolutely perfect, that must be much better than the guy who let it all pour out without blotting a line. You can get that resentment of the guy to whom it comes too easy in what Ben Jonson has to say about Shakespeare.

G: How does the process of your writing fiction fit in with your critical assessment of the evolution of literature?

F: Let me speak very personally. I think my own chief problem—and I don't feel very successful in my attempt—has been to escape my own bad training: I mean the training which I got originally which taught to respect the non-impulsive parts of writing more than the others. I feel as if I began locked out of the Garden and I've been banging at the gates ever since to try to get back in. Once in a while a story will come to me and write itself the way I think a story should.

G: Are you saying that you've changed your ideas about form: from an inclination toward highly arranged stories to a preference for evolving and dynamic—almost miasmic—stories?

F: I've spent a lot of time reading fairy tales, which I think of as pure story, very innocent story, trying to learn how you can release that again. I've been thinking about this problem a lot as I've been reading through Olaf Stapledon who is a very self-conscious writer in a way, yet every once in a while, when he's not looking, he'll let something slip by which just happened to him. I've just about finished reading all the way through Stapledon, and there's one book of his—*Sirius*—which he writes—without, I think, ever having been aware of it—one of the stories that's been told over and over and over again, the story of Beauty and the Beast. And in some ways, it's the most deeply moving story he ever wrote. He's an ice-cold writer, a contrived writer, most of the time, but it's the only story of his I ever read that I actually found myself moved to tears at the end of it.

G: What did you find moving? The fact that, in reinventing the wheel, so to speak, he had stepped outside of his artificial tendency towards order?

F: Right. I didn't have the feeling that he said to himself one day when his invention was flagging, "why don't I give a whirl to the old Beauty and the Beast story."

G: So he had innocently done it?

F: Yes, though in a different way, the way in which the story of Beauty and the Beast has to be written after Sigmund Freud. What's been fascinating me is how much Stapledon's version of Beauty and the Beast—with all of its superficial differences—is like *King Kong*, which is a very naive, almost contemporary, story.

G: Were you moved by the story of Beauty and the Beast or by Stapledon's telling of the story?

F: I was moved by the story which somehow he was innocent enough to let tell itself, to be faithful to itself. He didn't sit down and say, "Look, if I tell the story of Beauty and the Beast in the twentieth century, the beast can't turn into a human being at the end, he has to be hunted down by men and shot." That's the end of *King Kong* and that's the end of *Sirius*. The pathos of it is that we—all of us—have in some form or another (the story of Cupid and Psyche, the story of Beauty and the Beast, the story of the Frog Prince) some version of that story in our heads; and we know that it's a dream that doesn't work any more in a world where the maiden in the story is not a maiden—she's a non-virgin to begin with—so it blows up the whole thing.

G: Are you suggesting that stories transcend not only their literary context, but envelop the social context of the author, so that we read the story of an author writing a story as well as the larger climate that surrounds that whole process?

F: What I've been saying all along is the great thrill that you can get—at the stage we're at, where it's not usual any more and so many things work against it—is to see what happens when the story writes the writer.

G: Would you say that obsessive writers are among the most interesting writers?

F: I don't know how you can be a writer if you are not in some way obsessive.

G: What about a writer who writes the same book over and over?

F: There's a sense in which almost all writers do; there are damn few writers who really write brand new books. Melville is a pretty obsessive writer, a writer I like a lot. But an obsessive person can be a bore, right? And that's the risk for what I think of as the true, or obsessive, writer. I've been thinking of Isaac Bashevis Singer in those terms: he keeps writing the same damn story. Now Singer is lucky, you see, because Singer is the one writer who is widely respected in the late twentieth century who is, in some ways, absolutely unfallen—he's still connected with the naive roots of storytelling, folk storytelling. That's why he bugs, for instance, the more self-conscious Yiddish writers who thought they were delivered from all that shit of *Bobbeh meisseh*.

G: Simultaneously, isn't Singer's innocence something of a pose, a calculated refusal to be critical about his own storytelling?

F: Yes, it is. You have to say two things about Singer, one of which I just said. The other is that he's a devious son of a bitch. On the other hand, underneath all of his deviousness, there's a man who really is still connected to those stories. When he writes about those demons, it isn't because he sat down and said to himself, "You know, it would be good if somebody would still write about demons." He writes about them because he has to: he really is obsessed.

G: What constitutes the difference between the Singer story that chills one's soul and the story which one throws away as a piece of *shlak*? Is it the particular form he uses?

F: I don't think so. The answer I'm tempted to give isn't much help to anybody: when it works, it works; when it doesn't work, he fakes it. Singer is like most of the famous mediums were: they used to have real experiences sometimes, and when the experience didn't come, they faked it with yards of crepe and their accomplices in the next room. Sometimes you can see Singer working up the effect, and sometimes it just blessedly comes.

G: Is that where the danger involved with pure storytelling comes in: the telling of a story that is close to one's own psyche—when it works, it can be wonderful and thrilling, but at the same time, when it doesn't work, it can come perilously close to narcissism?

F: Oh, yes, and there's nothing worse than *faux naive*, you know—fake innocence is terrible. The storytellers that I'm talking about run two risks: one is that because they're obsessive they will turn into bores—they'll just end up *Haken a tsheinik* with the same old stuff over and over again; the other is that when their invention flags, they'll fake it.

G: Aside from Singer, which writers come to mind as examples of storytellers who at times "fake it"?

F: Let me talk about a writer I talk about a lot, and that people have very mixed feelings about, who is not taken nearly as seriously as Singer, although he's beginning to be (they've been discovering him in France recently), and this is Philip Farmer, the science fiction writer. He's now been discovered by the new French writers, and I have a novel by a young French experimental writer which just arrived in my mail the other day, called *Philip Farmer Conquers the Universe*, in which Philip Farmer becomes a mythological character in this guy's fiction.

G: Something like Joe Gores's novel, *Hammett?*

F: Yes.

G: Now, does Farmer compromise this innocence?

F: He's a man who must have written a hundred books by now, under various names—nobody knows exactly how many he's written, I don't think he remembers himself—and maybe in five of them, the thing really works. And the rest of the time, he does what he can. He also has the additional problem of being a man who earns a living by writing, so he's got to turn out a certain number of words a year; he doesn't have a university post or inherited money, but in some ways the professional writer has an advantage because if he keeps writing all the time, sooner or later he's going to tap back into the real vein.

G: Like a Norman Mailer?

F: Right, Mailer is very much like that, whereas the guy who says to himself to begin with, "I'm going to turn out two or three jewel-like works in my life and I'll burnish them and polish them and cut them until they're absolutely perfect": he can get into trouble, too. For example, William Gaddis has only written two books and one of them is not much good.

G: Are you referring to *J R* as the inferior work?

F: Yes. *The Recognitions* is a pain in the ass in some ways, but there's good stuff in it.

G: Would you say that *J R* is too cerebral?

F: Gaddis is pretty cerebral all the time, but it isn't even authentically cerebral any more: he's working it up.

G: So you feel that Gaddis wrote *J R* as opposed to it writing him?

F: Yes, that's right.

G: How would you say the writing of a nonfictional work is different from the writing of a fictional one?

F: I don't think it's very different, I really don't. The material is different, but if you think of a fiction as being a model of a certain experience, well then, one kind of fiction is what's called criticism: the only difference is that instead of being a model of the experience of love and death, it is a model of a model of that experience which already exists in Tolstoy's book, *War and Peace*, let's say.

G: Let me name a few characters from your novels—Mark Stone, Clem Stone, Baro Finkelstone, Jacob—as well as the many variations and personae of Leslie Fiedler which appear in your critical works: are you more attached to any one of these narrative selves?

F: The game I play (for reasons I don't quite understand) in my fiction is always to put somebody at the center of my fiction who I think of as being, in some absolutely fundamental way, totally different from myself but living through some of the same experiences. Whereas in my critical work, I'm always trying to invent a fictional mouthpiece who is as close to my *real* self—whatever the hell that is—as possible. I think I distance myself more in fiction. I think I'm much more successful in short stories than in my novels. As far as my own feelings about what I've done, I think very early I wrote a story which I think of as one I would have liked to write ideally, a little, tiny story which is called "The Teeth." And I think, again, I wrote a successful story in "Nobody Ever Died From It": I'm moved by that when I read it now, at a distance, when it seems like the work of somebody else. The longest thing that I ever wrote that really worked for me is "Nude Croquet."

G: What appeals to you about these stories? "Nude Croquet," especially, seems to me to be a highly arranged piece of work, rather in the manner you earlier suggested you are moving away from. Nonetheless, it is a poignant story.

F: Of all my fictions, "Nude Croquet" is the one which most wrote itself and which is least dependent upon experiences I happen to have lived through—the whole game was sheer invention: I've never played a game of nude croquet; I've never witnessed a game of nude croquet—and especially, the ending wrote itself.

G: Was it the innate comic aspect of the story which took over?

F: I think I'm essentially a comic writer, anyhow. I arranged the story so that the comic poignance could come free. That's where arrangement comes into play. Sometimes arrangement just turns out to be for its own sake, other times not. Another story of mine which released simultaneously pathos and comedy without cancelling each other out is "The Last Jew in America."

G: If we're to have a model for this, perhaps we might return to your comments on *Ulysses* where you cited a multitude of conscious and unconscious forces but the unconscious aspects are able to emerge without hindrance.

F: I think that writers who begin with—or are trained into—hyperconsciousness, sometimes need to arrange things so that once they get everything arranged there is space for the deep stuff to emerge: arrangement clears space. My unpublished story—which I hope to God will come along one of these days if ever Harlan Ellison does anything with the collection—is a story called "What Used to be Called Dead"; it's a story which in some ways will look to you like the most unnatural and contrived and artificial and almost, one would think, *chic* story I've ever written; on the other hand, I think of it as—and it is—the most spontaneous story I've ever written: I wrote it without thought; whatever arrangement is there was done by a force beyond my control.

G: For me, all of your fiction seems to be arranged around a visionary scene that takes its shape as the culmination of the particular fictional scenario; the plot leads up to this scene, but the vision—almost like a mystical experience—encompasses and transcends the plot progression.

F: That sounds right to me. I don't know whether I would have said it myself, but when you say it, I find myself agreeing. In the stories that I'm talking about, it's the vision of what it really means to be naked in "Nude Croquet," or, at the end of "Nobody Ever Died From It," it's the kid's first vision that betrayal is not something that other people do to you but what everybody does to everybody and which you do to yourself. Or the *Kol Nidre* in "The Last Jew in America." The story seems to be a way of getting to a place where vision is available to me. I don't begin with a vision and then work the story around it; the story works itself to the point where the vision is released—that only happens through the story.

G: Would you say that all your stories are "meditations" in the same way that *Freaks* is?

F: The most mythological story I ever wrote is the one that's most nearly a pure meditation: that's the story I call "The Dancing of Reb Hershl with the Withered Hand." You know, it occurs to me that the way you've described my stories could be said to apply to Stapledon—except he does it too deliberately. All his stories end with a vision.

G: When I speak of vision, I mean a transcendent vision: the nude croquet game exists, everything leads up to it, but a different plot would lead up to it as well. Towards the end, Howard is recognizing the arbitrary quality of the plot—he doesn't quite remember whether he had sex with the young wife of the host and what else happened exactly—but he does know and participate in, as does everyone else, the nude croquet game—and it is that experience which prevails.

F: Yes. I actually began to write the story because somebody told me about a nude croquet game. And then I did this "what if": what if I imagined a game of nude croquet and put such-and-such kind of people in it, how would it come out? The point of the story was to explore what would happen: I didn't know what was going to happen; I knew what I wanted to put together in order to see what would happen.

G: You once commented about John Hawkes that he "makes terror rather than love the center of his work, knowing all the while, of course, that there can be no terror without the hope for love and love's defeat." Might it be said of Leslie Fiedler that he made boundaries the center of his work, knowing all the while that there can be no boundaries without the hope for unity and unity's defeat?

F: Ay-yi-yi, you saved a great question for last! I'm not sure. The word "boundaries" surprised me: I don't think of myself in that way. I think of innocence as being at the heart of the thing. And then there's another funny theme which is in my stories and always surprises me when I discover how prominent it is there, and that's the question of identity, in a very special way: whose child is whose? That's sort of a compulsive theme in my stories. Begetting and children are real important to me. It's in *Back to China*, it's in *Freaks*, too—it's played out in various kinds of ways. The boundaries of identity are always with me. Did he fuck this girl, or that girl, or who's the father, or who's the son? I suppose I think of boundaries in the sense of terminal boundaries: beginnings and ends, and the fading of ends into beginnings. Maybe it's the ambiguity of the negative which interests me more than anything: the yes that's under the no, the beginning that's under the end. In a funny way, I think of myself as a secret affirmative writer pretending to be a nihilist. I know that someplace there are absolute categories; I equally know that we never perceive them.

G: Would you like to?

F: I think so, but since I've never tried it, how can I say for sure? That's the dream: maybe I'm only teased by it because I know that it's always just out of my grasp. You know, those visions at the end of the stories are, in a way, momentary glimpses of a place where the contradictions are all resolved.

G: Would that be innocence?

F: Yes, that would be the reestablishment of innocence.

Generic Geographies

Jackson I. Cope
University of Southern California

Let us begin by listening to the metaphors.

"How many trees make up a forest? How many houses a city? . . . as the Germanic proverb goes, one cannot see the forest for the trees. Forest and city are two things essentially deep, and depth is fatally condemned to become a surface if it wants to be visible."

"I have fixed my attention chiefly on temporal depth, which is the past, and spatial depth, which is distance. But both are only examples, special cases of depth. What does depth consist of, taken *in genere?*"

Ortega y Gasset's metaphors for movement, for the human placed, standing, in time, in that creation which is, after all, simply his imagining, as if it were just this forest, not quite platonic, not quite place:

"Literary genres are, then, the poetic functions, the directions, in which esthetic creation moves."

"In one way or another man is always the essential theme of art, and the genres understood as mutually exclusive esthetic themes, equally essential and final, are wide vistas seen from the main sides of human nature. Each epoch brings with it a basic interpretation of man. Or rather, the epoch does not bring the interpretation with it but actually *is* such an interpretation. For this reason, each epoch prefers a particular genre."

From the opening forest, he returns at the close of the *Meditations on Quixote* to that river which had introduced the idea of perspectivism in the first essays in *El espectador*:

"Every literary genre . . . is a river-bed which one of these interpretations of man has opened up, nothing is less surprising than the preference of each epoch for a particular genre."[1]

Geographies: "forests," "cities," "river beds," — depths and surfaces. Another direction in which to write literary history; yet literary history recognizably traditional. The context of contacts among works, authors, influences and coincidences made internal, structural as it is turned into metaphor, become generic as it turns outward. It is in this simple sense that one maps these geographies.

"Geography," the OED explains, is "the science that describes the earth's surface, its forms and physical features, its natural and political divisions, its climates, productions." Add a rider from Northrop Frye's version of the relation between fictional narrative and its forebears: "the bumps and hollows of the story being told follow the contours of the myth beneath."[2] With these reminders one can review the metaphoric bonding between the form and history of what period-minded critics call variously modern, post-modern, contemporary fiction; what others have called experimental, or metafiction or surfiction to distinguish it from the "novel" as a familiar genre.

As in Victorian life, in Victorian literature the vision of a wasted and despairing city created in the imagination's merger of industrialism and Dante seems ubiquitous. Reviewing Alexander Smith's early poems, Clough suggested that they seemed to satisfy the need for a new poetry giving beauty to "the black streams that welter out of factories, the dreary lengths of urban and suburban dustiness." Indeed, "There are moods when one is prone to believe that, in these last days, no longer by 'clear spring or shady grove' . . . are the true and lawful haunts of the poetic powers; but . . . if anywhere, in the blank and desolate streets, and upon the solitary bridges of the midnight city, where Guilt is . . . and pale Hope, that looks like Despair."[3] We have been well-taught the complexity of Dickens' historical yet metaphoric cities, but Gissing's London slums were more characteristic in their openly Dantesque violence: "this place to which you are confined is Hell! There is no escape for you . . . at the end there is waiting for you, one and all, a death in abandonment and despair. This is Hell—Hell—Hell!"[4] Later Virginia Woolf, that great misunderstander of Gissing, was equally aware with Eliot of invoking Dante for a more modern London: "this city we travel . . . Leave there to perish your hope . . . Bare are the pillars; auspicious to none . . . 'Good night, good night. You go this way?' 'Alas. I go that.' "[5]

The young James Joyce learned from the Victorians much better than Woolf how to turn some brilliant glimpses of the turn-of-the-century Dublin scene into the first collection of stories ordered as a metaphor of the modern psyche. He meant it in a structural sense when he wrote of titling "the series *Dubliners* to betray the soul of that hemiplegia or paralysis which many consider a city."[6] The metaphor became increasingly woven into the work, of course, to become the fibre for the development of both plot and character in *Finnegans Wake*, after having served as the complex grid map of *Ulysses*.[7]

The city is in one sense a confine; in another, an extension, expression of the individual defined socially. But it constitutes a temporal confinement different in quality from the mystery which is race, culture, even a continent when place is realized as mirror of the psychic environment. And both are different from the self-definition realized in the shell, the home as haven or prison. And if Joyce (we sometimes forget that he grew up a Victorian) wove the city ever more thickly into his modern tapestry, his quondam protégè Samuel Beckett (and who better to identify as the progenitor of contemporary fiction?) narrowed the formal metaphor to the room, repeatedly measuring the spirit against the limited dimensions of its container, whether in *Film*, in the enclosure of *The Lost Ones* ("Seen from below the wall presents an unbroken surface all the way round and up to the ceiling. . . . Lying down is unheard of in the cylinder. . . . Such privation is partly to be explained by the dearth of floor space namely a little under one square metre at the disposal of each body") or in the M trilogy:

> I am in my mother's room. It is I who live there now. I don't know how I got there. . . . Present state. This room seems to be mine. I can find no other explanation to my being left in it. All this time. . . . Perhaps I came in for the room on the death of whoever was in it before me.[8]

But even as Beckett was reducing the geography of fictional form to the space of a little room, in Latin America fiction was emerging into a more expansive maturity. "The continent has dawned on them as unwritten history," observed Alistair Reid of Asturias, Borges and the younger generation embracing Cortázar, Garcia Márquez, Fuentes and the others who have been forging a new post-Spanish fiction during the past three decades.[9]

But forging it from the stuff of an old problem, promise, articulated in different terms by their predecessors, the strain from Sarmiento to Gallegos to Onetti which reveals "the radical uncertainty about the role of the city, . . . found in the very origins of the realist novel."[10] The city versus the virgin continent early emerged in Latin-American fiction as a sociological division which becomes reconciled through metaphor in Asturias' *Hombres de maiz* (1949). In that novel he transplanted Mayan mythology from the *Popol vuh* which had already been used in *El sẽnor presidente* (1946) to give the urban nightmare of corrupt political dictatorship a demi-causal relation to mythic rumblings fueling the modern inferno.

Borges, however, stood aside from the sub-continent's mood of political and ethnic interweaving just far enough to adapt and expand its spatial metaphors into infinitudes of imaginary place, cities more real but no less precisely abstract than the invisible ones projected in Italo Calvino's distilled 'European' meditation.

Borges has been obsessed with the possibilities of geometry become geography from the first fictions and inquisitions. The Library of Babel is as precisely plotted in its infinite orders as the room of Beckett's M. And the encyclopedic invention by an imaginary Rosicrucian group of an entire third universe with its own rules of logic and its own geography ("Tlön, Uqbar, Orbis Tertius") is a triumph of the passion for breaking through the phenomenal orders we assume in nature to create a new landscape with the imagination: "Tlön may be a labyrinth, but it is a labyrinth plotted by men, a labyrinth destined to be deciphered by men."[11] It is an interior geography, but one which interiorizes continents only to expand them again. As Borges says of the geography of cabbalistic geometrics in "Death and the Compass," the crime "occurs in a Buenos Aires of dreams: the twisted Rue de Toulon is the Paseo de Julio. . . . After composing the narrative, I have come to consider the soundness of amplifying the time and space in which it occurs . . . the periods of time might be computed in years, perhaps in centuries; the first letter of the Name might be spoken in Iceland; the second, in Mexico; the third in Hindustan" (*Ficciones*, p. 105). This is a rare glimpse into an author's return to the decomposition of his own fictional structure, a return which boasts his capacity for expanding the universe to those extreme limits marking the liberties of his imagination. One might hear echoes of Borges' interest in the Renaissance imagination particularized by John Donne ("You . . . Who did the whole world's soul contract, and drove / Into the glasses of your eyes . . . Countries, towns, courts"). Yet, the phenomenon has its counterparts in numerous sitings within the the "other," "sociological" literature of Latin America.

Julio Cortázar, self-styled "argentino afrancesado," for one instance, redeployed the expanding geographies suggested by his Argentinian compatriot in the twinned "travel" novels (*Hopscotch* and *62: A Model Kit*) which retrace Argentina in Paris and Paris in Argentina. But it is Miguel Angél Asturias and Gabriel Garcia Márquez who have been writing most literally the unwritten history of the South American continent; Asturias most exemplarily, perhaps, in the relatively late *Mulata* (1963) which is an earlier analogue (and in part, no doubt, inspiration) to Garcia Márquez's *One Hundred Years of Solitude*. Asturias's myth laminates the spirit and shape of the land boldly. The book begins with the comic erotic grotesque of a village Faust who sells souls and wife to the daemonic Tazol, the wife being taken up in a whirlwind at the beginning, even as Garcia Márquez' 'Macondo' will disappear in a whirlwind at the end. The Mayan sources gradually dominate the rabelaisian village adventures as the figures become metaphoric, demimythological creatures; themselves become the protagonists of their old mythologies; finally become the mountains, moon and clouds constituting the furthest origins of the myths. The myths deepen in fantasy as Christian and pagan cultures clash in a metaphoric war which explodes in a cataclysm of earthquake and flood creating that natural (and literal) landscape in which the whole is set: Guatemala itself:

" . . . hills and valleys in soapy waves were pushed against the grain by serpentine fissures that flowed along roads torn out like pieces of hairy skin, along with the breaking of bubbling water that ran to hide itself from the moon . . . 'Ding, dong, ding . . . sexton, sing, where are the bells, make them ring!' "

"He raised his eyes to the sky . . . not a cloud . . . indigo . . . completely indigo . . . not even stars . . . barely visible in the powerful nearby light of the moon that was about to fall and where, judging from the shaking of the earth, it was still quaking. . . "

"A total muteness. Not only of what is communication, tongue, language, speech, song, noise. . . . The silence, the silence itself was also silent between the earth and the sky, while the day painted itself along with immense feathers of fire, along which, on even more luminous grooves, furrows of little colored feathers ran as they piled up, pushed by who knows what wind, toward the place where Tierrapaulita had been and was only buried, and from which Father Chimalpín could not take away his eyes, as if from looking into the midst of that sea of tumbled mountains, from staring and staring at the same spot, his eyes were able to penetrate toward the bottom until they found it . . . and he preferred to cross himself, but when he raised his arm, his hand was lost in the air, it did not reach his forehead, it fell apart on him, it was not there, just as the mule was not there either and had left no trace."[12]

In Garcia Márquez's fiction the same sort of cycling through time into cataclysms by which geographical place is developed and destroyed takes a scriptural turn as the generations spiral in repetition of one another within the village of Macondo somewhere beyond the uncrossable sea. *Cien años*: both title and metaphor, because as the repetitive history of the Buendía family who founded Macondo proceeds, much greater times elapse: somehow we span from Drake to the daguerreotype, and ages become merely mythic upon the analogy of the enormous genealogies of the Old Testament. And, in the end, it is again geographic place which is at the center of form: when Macondo collapses into a necropolis, *One Hundred Years of Solitude* is completed. Reading the gypsy manuscript which is both prophecy and history of the myth of the village, the last Buendía recognizes it as, paradoxically, the history of Joyce's city, of a continent, even, compressed finally into a little room:

> Only then did he discover . . . that Sir Francis Drake had attacked Riohacha only so that they could seek each other through the most intricate labyrinths of blood until they would engender the mythical animal that was to bring the line to an end. Macondo was already a fearful whirlwind of dust and rubble being spun about by the wrath of the biblical hurricane when Aureliano skipped eleven pages . . . to anticipate the predictions and ascertain the date and circumstances of his death. Before reaching the final line, however, he had already understood that he would never leave that room, for it was foreseen that the city of mirrors (or mirages) would be wiped out by the wind and exiled from the memory of men at the precise moment when Aureliano Babilonia would finish deciphering the parchments.[13]

The bridges seem innumerable as they reconnect fictions across continents and imaginative premises. One of the earliest enduring underground classics, Malcolm Lowry's *Under the Volcano*, takes its structure from overlaying the mystical symbolism of the ancient cabbala upon that contemporary Mexico from which Lowry derived so much of his inspiration. In a letter which must rank as one of the most eccentric explications ever offered by an author as commentary upon his own fiction, Lowry explained to Jonathan Cape that

> the deeply buried layer of the novel or poem that attaches itself to myth, does so to the Jewish Cabbala. . . . The Cabbala is used for poetical purposes

because it represents man's spiritual aspiration. . . . The scene is Mexico, the meeting place, according to some, of mankind itself. . . . Its geographical remoteness from us, as well as the closeness of its problems to our own, will assist the tragedy each in its own way. We can see it as the world itself, or the Garden of Eden, or both at once. Or we can see it as a kind of timeless symbol of the world on which we can place the Garden of Eden, the Tower of Babel and indeed anything else we please.[14]

Lowry goes on chapter by chapter to explain the various cabbalistic details of the alcoholic Consul's last adventure "under the volcano." Indeed, when the protagonist "shows Hugh his alchemistic books . . . we are for a moment, . . . standing before the evidence of what is no less than the magical basis of the world" (p. 76). Everywhere this magic permeates Lowry's Mexico: "the whole Tlaxcala business *does* have an underlying deep seriousness. Tlaxcala, of course, just like Parián, is death: but the Tlaxcalans were Mexico's traitors—here the Consul is giving way to the forces within him that are betraying himself" (p. 82). It is not so arbitrary a connection as at first might appear, since Lowry interprets the mystic tradition in such a manner as to make the protagonist himself a metaphoric extension of this, his mythic place:

> In the Cabbala, the misuse of magical powers is compared to drunkenness or the misuse of wine, and termed, if I remember rightly, in Hebrew *sōd*, . . . There is a kind of attribute of the word *sōd* also which implies garden or a neglected garden. (p. 71)

The Consul's house garden has been allowed to go to disreputable seed along with his psyche, imaging the latter in a way made less simple not only by these extra-textual commentaries, but by the omnipresence of the public garden of Quauhnahuac, that town which lies under the volcano to epitomize (as the opening paragraph of the novel makes clear) the varied places of this world: "It is situated well south of the Tropic of Cancer, to be exact on the nineteenth parallel, in about the same latitude as the Revillagigedo Islands to the west in the Pacific, or very much further west, the southernmost tip of Hawaii—and as the port of Tzucox to the east on the Atlantic seaboard of Yucatan near the border of British Honduras, or very much further east, the town of Juggernaut, in India, on the Bay of Bengal."[15] It is to this last integer of the geographic equation that the whole has been tending, of course; its intention to bridge that brief space across which place can become myth, a symbol freed of origin. Juggernaut: the deity beneath the wheels of whose wagon the sacrificial victims are hurled to be crushed. And even as the Consul lies dying beneath the volcano in Mexico, his vision is of mountains simultaneously there and in India: "He was in Kashmir, he knew, lying in the meadows near running water among violets and trefoil, the Himalayas beyond, which made it all the more remarkable that he should suddenly be setting out . . . to climb Popocatepetl" (p. 374). But the ascent is mirage, an inverted dream image of the Consul's nightmare of the final fall:

> there was nothing there: no peaks, no life, no climb . . . he was falling, fall-
> ing into the volcano . . . the world itself was bursting, bursting into black
> spouts of villages catapulted into space, with himself falling through it all.
> . . . Somebody threw a dead dog after him down the ravine. (p. 375)

These are the last words of narrative in *Under the Volcano*, yet not the last words—which are closure as commentary. If the Consul himself is an untended garden, it is Mexico from which he is expelled, a place no different from those other homes of judgement, Juggernaut. In the public garden of Quauhnahuac there is a sign which occupies a final page, capitalized to underline its function as epigraph to the fiction, epitaph to the Consul and fallen man: "¿LE GUSTA ESTE JARDÍN / QUE ES SUYO? / ¡EVITE QUE SUS HIJOS LO DESTRUYAN!" Much earlier "The Consul stared back at the black words on the sign without moving. You like this garden? Why is it yours? We evict those who destroy! Simple words, simple and terrible words . . . per- haps a final judgement on one" (p. 128). Lowry's letter implicitly ex- plains why, as he says, his protagonist here "slightly mistranslates." It is in order that the full irony of self-expulsion can be kept in abeyance for the epigraph (*Letters*, p. 74): "The allegory is that of the Garden of Eden, the Garden representing the world, from which we ourselves run perhaps slightly more danger of being ejected than when I wrote the book. The drunkenness of the Consul is used on one plane to symbolize the universal drunkenness of mankind during the war, or during the period immediately preceding it . . . his fate should be seen also in its universal relationship to the ultimate fate of mankind" (p. 66).

The naked simplicity of Lowry's commentary combines with the permanent respect accorded *Under the Volcano* to make it the paradoxic- ally "American classic" of that fiction of mythic places I am describing. Paradoxical because neither Lowry nor the Consul was "American," Lowry having made a pilgrimage from England to Boston which led on to Hollywood, Mexico and Vancouver in order to meet Conrad Aiken, the American novelist whose *Blue Voyage* Lowry "knew . . . by heart. Its influence on him was profound and permanent."[16]

This may remind us of my initial remarks about a literary history of new fiction which will utilize geographic leaps, connections and metaphors as generic clues, forms. What is the literary "nationality" of that other traveller from Europe in a metaphoric America, the Nabokov of *Lolita*? We know that Borges was not only bilingual from childhood, but bicultural in our context, having spent so much time in the United States on a species of academic shuttle system—which is to say nothing of his German and French history. But what is the literary language of Beckett? What is the "native" tradition of Asturias, of Cortázar, of Goytisolo—all writing Spanish so long from their bases in France? These are (in one of our favorite metaphors for the artist's relation to his milieu) "rooted," respectively, in Anglo-Irish and Hispanic culture, literature, mythologies. But they have flourished (to recall a common extension of the organic metaphor) in France at a moment when significant French voices have addressed the problematics of literary and cultural space. From this chorus let us select here only the voice of the truest poet.

Generic relationships flower into visible fields of historic pattern; their generations rise and fade even as those of the Buendías in Macondo. In the particular fictions whose form we are pursuing the inner life is perceived as place, as small as the room, as grandiose as the continent, until time itself is recognized as swept up into the pattern of imagined spaces. In gathering these inter-related metaphors into an instructive cluster, Jean Genet's prison fiction presents itself as paradigm and epitome. Inevitable, it seems, that for Genet "place" should be a metaphor for the paradisaical, that "new" place which returns to the oldest mythic significance of the self in society, where society is nothing more nor less than the inner commune of the self imagining its own dissemination: "If he was kind . . . it was that he might offer me a hospitality which was to fulfill utterly my most secret desires . . . which are the only ones that can make of me the finest of characters, that is, the one most identical with myself. I aspire to Guiana. No longer to that geographical place now depopulated and emasculated, but to the proximity, the promiscuity, not in space but in consciousness, of the sublime models, the great archetypes of misfortune"; "I would like to make a bouquet of these handsome boys . . . they might flower, bloom and offer me the revels which are the pride of my ideal Guiana."[17] (In the *Meditations*, Ortega y Gasset had realized in theory Genet's practice: "The 'meaning' of a thing is the highest form of its coexistence with other things—it is its depth dimension. . . . Meditation is an erotic exercise: the concept, an amorous rite" [p. 89]). But these boys are not objects: they are projections like Guiana itself of a wished-for flowering which is wistful; masculine desire for expression of something which seems forever incommunicable because of its very power: "The males are dependent only upon themselves. They are their own heaven, and, knowing their weakness, they hesitate . . . the men, the toughs . . . were composed of a kind of feminine fog in which I would still like to lose myself so that I might feel more intensely that I was a solid block" (p. 59). A flowering, then, into the image and reflection of a place and its once present, now imaginatively-heightened inhabitants. But a flowering in which the dreamer's male voice becomes metaphor for the feminine certitude of creation without renouncing its masculine burden of doubt about the possibility of closure as an act of the self. These are metaphors spawned by the world Michel Foucault has described as systematic incarceration,[18] by Genet's literal prison experience itself made metaphoric. And we are back to the terrible geography of modern life raised to the courage of Beckett's sojourner in a little room: "you must go on, you can't go on, I'll go on." But back, too, to Guiana, to imagination encompassing continents.

Claudio Guillén, studying the influence of influence as a unifying factor in the birth of modern literary history from an atomistic nineteenty-century poetics, reminds us that "The concept of the nation, regarded by definition as an organic whole, growing and developing in history, became the all-embracing principle of unity."[19] With the critical bankruptcy of such a history it would seem that we must give up the traditional sense of periodicity and place (created by the slower processes of interchange, of translation and travel in the pre-World War II millenia), replacing, relocating it with a new geography connecting affinities within a body of fiction paradoxically grounded in the primacy of place. We would have something roughly similar to what Guillén himself calls a "system": "historical constellations, lasting and yet constantly moving, ideal spaces with which the practicing writer has to come to terms" (pp. 7–8).

Such a "system" would constitute our critical response and homage to a recognition by most of the most creative contemporary fictionists that they can discern more clearly than before the myths and metaphors which clarify the bumps and hollows of their own culture because they can see it from another place, from the network of connected visions which they share with those others who are writing the history of "the contours of the myth beneath" their original and ultimately radical cultural and physical geography.

Not sources, then, but sitings. Messages across and about the inner shape of continents, the shape of interiorized spaces, places as metaphor for the shape of thought.

NOTES

1. José Ortega y Gasset, *Meditations on Quixote*, trans. E. Rugg and D. Marín (1914; New York, 1963), pp. 59, 87, 112–13, 151.

2. *A Natural Perspective: The Development of Shakespearean Comedy and Romance* (Princeton, 1965), p. 61.

3. *Poems and Prose Remains* (London, 1869), I, 362–63 (first published 1853).

4. *The Nether World*, cited in J. A. V. Chapple, *Documentary and Imaginary Literature, 1880–1920* (New York, 1970), p. 96.

5. "The String Quartet" (1921) in *The Haunted House* (London, 1944), pp. 22–27. Alexander Welsh, *The City of Dickens* (Oxford, 1971) offers indispensable illumination upon the tradition.

6. *Letters*, ed. Stuart Gilbert (New York, 1966), I, 55.

7. I have expanded these observations in the first chapter of *Joyce's Cities: Archaeologies of the Soul* (Baltimore, 1981).

8. *The Lost Ones* (New York, 1972), pp. 55, 60; *Molloy* and *Malone Dies* in *Three Novels* (New York, 1955), pp. 7, 182–83.

9. "Basilisks' Eggs" (a review of Marcia Márquez) in *The New Yorker*, Nov. 8, 1976, p. 177.

10. Gordon Brotherton, *The Emergence of the Latin American Novel* (Cambridge, 1977), p. 12. Cf. the insistence upon continent as metaphor in Carpentier (pp. 15–16, 45–59), in Onetti (pp. 64–65), and in Cortázar (pp. 81–97).

11. Jorge Luis Borges, *Ficciones*, ed. Anthony Kerrigan (New York, 1962), p. 34.

12. Miguel Angel Asturias, *Mulata*, trans. Gregory Rabassa (New York, 1967), pp. 292–93, 305–06.

13. *One Hundred Years of Solitude*, trans. Gregory Rabassa (1967; New York, 1971), p. 383.

14. Malcolm Lowry, *Selected Letters*, ed. Harvey Breit and Margerie Bonner Lowry (Philadelphia and New York, 1965), pp. 65–67.

15. *Under the Volcano* (1947; New York, 1965), p. 3.

16. Conrad Aiken, "Malcolm Lowry: A Note," in *Malcolm Lowry: Psalms and Songs*, ed. Margerie Lowry (New York, 1975), p. 57.

17. *The Thief's Journal*, trans. Bernard Frechtman (1949; New York, 1973), pp. 254–55.

18. *Histoire de la Folie* (1961); and *Surveiller et Punir; Naissance de la prison* (1975).

19. *Literature as System: Essays Toward the Theory of Literary History* (Princeton, 1971), p. 5.

INDEX

Abish, Walter: 24
Ada (Nabokov): 23
Aeneid (Virgil): 103
"Aesthetics of Silence, The" (Sontag): 9–13
Africa, The (Petrarca): 2
Aiken, Conrad: 159
Ambler, Eric: 40–42
American Review: 59
Anarchiad (Humphreys): 103
Apuleius Madaurensis: 131n.3
Ariosto, Lodovico: 2
Aristotle: 2–3, 5, 16, 104
Artaud, Antonin: 12, 15
"Art in a Closed Field" (Kenner): 35
Asturias, Miguel: 153, 154, 155, 159

"Baby-Sitter, The" (Coover): 5–8
Background to Danger (Ambler): 40–42
Back to China (Fiedler): 128
Balzac, Honoré de: 27, 140
Barlow, Joel: 106
Barth, John: 7, 23, 25, 27, 95–115
Barthelme, Donald: 7, 18, 27
Barthes, Roland: 11, 13, 14, 16, 17, 27, 28, 68
Bataille, Georges: 12
Baudelaire, Charles: 113
Beckett, Samuel: 13, 26, 47, 153, 154, 159, 160
Bellow, Saul: 25
Benjamin, Walter: 14
Berger, Thomas: 107
Berger Extravagant, Le (Sorel): 15
Bernal, J. D.: 20
Bernstein, Bob: 61
Big Sky (Guthrie): 107
Birth of Tragedy, The (Nietzsche): 140
"Black Monk, The" (Chekov): 43
Blake, William: 15
Blanchot, Maurice: 14
Blue Voyage (Aiken): 159
Boccaccio, Giovanni: 2, 3
Böll, Heinrich: 26
Booth, Wayne: 79–80
Borges, Jorge Luis: 37–38, 43, 55, 80, 89, 109, 134, 153, 154, 159
Braak, Ter: 14
Brant, Joseph: 106
Brautigan, Richard: 18
Brighton Rock (Greene): 40
Broch, Hermann: 15
Brusati, Franco: 69
Buenos Aires Affair (Puig): 7
Burroughs, William: 10, 12, 13

Cage, John: 10, 11, 12
Caillois, Roger: 57
Calvino, Italo: 7, 26, 43, 47, 54, 113, 154
Campanella, Tommaso: 2
Camus, Albert: 35
Cape, Jonathan: 156
Carter, Angela: 47
Castelvetro, Lodovico: 2
Castle of Crossed Destinies, The (Calvino): 54
"Cat in the Hat for President, The": see *Political Fable, A*
Catch 22 (Heller): 35
Centaur, The (Updike): 81–82
Centennial (Michener): 107
Cervantes, Miguel: 2, 3, 19, 95, 97, 108, 109, 113
Chambers, George: 24
Chandler, Raymond: 34
Chardin, Teilhard de: 19
Charlie in the House of Rue (Coover): 46, 63
Chaucer, Geoffrey: 17
Chekov, Anton: 43
Chimera (Barth): 95, 97, 101, 104
Clough, Arthur: 152
Cockburn, Lord: 106
Confessions of Nat Turner, The (Styron): 107
Conroy, Frank: 79–80, 82–86
Coover, Robert: 1, 5–8, 25, 45–63, 107
Cortázar, Julio: 153, 154, 155, 159
Cosmicomics (Calvino): 26, 113
Cross, Mary Ann Evans: see Eliot, George
Cummings, E. E.: 20n.3

"Dancing of Reb Hershl with the Withered Hand, The" (Fiedler): 148
Daniel Deronda (Eliot): 65
Daniel Martin (Fowles): 65–78
Dante: 152
Davis, Dlyde Brian: 103
Davis, Robert Gorham: 34
"Death and Rebirths of the Novel, The" (Fiedler): 137, 139
"Death and the Compass" (Borges): 154
Decameron (Boccaccio): 2
"Deserters: The Contemporary Defeat of Fiction, The" (Oglesby): 35
Dickens, Charles: 152
Doctorow, E. L.: 107
Donatus: 2
Donne, John: 154
Don Quixote (Cervantes): 2, 19, 97, 108, 113
Drake, Francis: 156
Dubliners, The (Joyce): 153
Duchamp, Marcel: 15

Durkheim, Émile: 57

Eisenhower, Dwight D.: 58
"Elevator, The" (Coover): 54
Eliot, George (Mary Ann Evans Cross): 65
Eliot, T. S.: 14, 15, 113, 152
Ellison, Harlan: 147
End of the Road, The (Barth): 25, 98, 104
End to Innocence, An (Fiedler): 135, 136
Espectador, El (Ortega y Gasset): 151
Evans, Mary Ann: see Eliot, George
Exley, Frederick: 79–80, 82–92

Fan's Notes, A (Exley): 82–92
Farmer, Philip: 144–45
Faulkner, William: 15, 23, 46, 113, 140
"Fear of Innocence, The" (Fiedler): 136
Federman, Raymond: 7, 27
Felix Holt the Radical (Eliot): 65
Fiddlehead, The: 52
Fiedler, Leslie A.: 7, 133–49
Fielding, Henry: 3
Film (Beckett): 153
Finnegans Wake (Joyce): 153
Flaubert, Gustave: 17, 113, 141
Flight to Canada (Reed): 107
Floating Opera, The (Barth): 97, 104
Foucault, Michel: 160
Fowles, John: 65–78, 91–92
Franklin, Benjamin: 79
Freaks (Fiedler): 147, 148
French Lieutenant's Woman, The (Fowles): 91–92
Freud, Sigmund: 55, 142
Frye, Northrop: 14, 18, 152
Fuentes, Carlos: 153
Fuller, Buckminster: 19

Gaddis, William: 23, 145
Gallegos Freire, Rómulo: 153
Gardner, John: 25, 51
Gass, William: 7, 25
Gelber, Jack: 53
Genet, Jean: 159–60
Genre: 1
Gide, Andre: 18, 113
Gilabert, Henri: 53
Giles Goat-Boy (Barth): 97, 98
Gissing, George: 152
God: 19
Goethe, Johann Wolfgang von: 110
Golden Ass, The (Apuleius Madaurensis): 131n.3
Gombrich, Ernst Hans: 55
Gombrowicz, Witold: 48
Gores, Joseph: 145
Gottlieb, Bob: 60
Goytisolo, Juan: 159

Grass, Günter: 26, 47
Gravity's Rainbow (Pynchon): 23, 25
"Great American Novel–, The" (Davis): 103
Great American Novel, The (Roth): 103
Great American Novel, The (Williams): 103, 110
Green, Geoffrey: 1
Greene, Graham: 40
Guarini, Giovanni Battista: 2
Guillén, Claudio: 160
Guinzburg, Tom: 61
Guthrie, Alfred: 107

Haley, Alex: 107
Hamlet (Shakespeare): 3
Hammett (Gores): 145
Handman, Wynn: 53
Hassan, Ihab: 13, 14, 15–16, 18, 19, 20
Hathaway, Baxter: 2
Hawkes, John: 7, 25, 39–42, 45, 104, 117–32, 140, 148
Hawthorne, Nathaniel: 86
Heller, Joseph: 25, 35, 36
Hemingway, Ernest: 15, 133
Hildesheimer, Wolfgang: 39
Hoffman, E. T. A.: 113
Hoffmannsthal, von Hugo: 15
Hombres de maís (Asturias): 154
Homer: 2
Hoover, J. Edgar: 58
Hopscotch (Cortázar): 155
Humphreys, David: 103

Il pastor fido (Guarini): 2
Invisible Cities (Calvino): 26

James, Henry: 14, 71, 110, 139
Janvier, Ludovic: 25
Jarry, Alfred: 15, 113
Johns, Jasper: 10
Johnson, Samuel: 141
Jonson, Ben: 141
Joyce, James: 3, 14, 15, 26, 65, 79–80, 113, 138, 139–40, 152–53, 156
JR (Gaddis): 23, 145

Kafka, Franz: 15, 26, 48, 113
Katz, Steve: 24
Kenner, Hugh: 35
"Kid, The" (Coover): 53, 54
King Kong: 142–43
Krieger, Murray: 16
Kristeva, Julia: 11–12, 19

"Last Jew in America, The" (Fiedler): 147
Lautréamont (Isidore Ducasse): 11, 15
Lawrence, D. H.: 15, 72, 75, 140
Lazarillo de Tormes: 108
Lazarillo de Tormes: see Life of Lazarillo de Tormes, The

Letters (Barth): 23, 27, 95–115
Lewis, Clive Staples: 14
Lie Down in Darkness (Faulkner): 23
Life of Lazarillo de Tormes, The (Lazarillo de Tormes): 108
Lime Twig, The (Hawkes): 39–42
"Literature of Exhaustion, The" (Barth): 111–12
"Literature of Replenishment: Post-modernist Fiction, The" (Barth): 111–13
Little Big Man (Berger): 107
Litz, Walton: 3, 7
Lodge, David: 17
Lolita (Nabokov): 139–40, 159
Lost in the Funhouse (Barth): 95ff.
Lost Ones, The (Beckett): 153
Love and Death in the American Novel (Fiedler): 135
"Love Scene" (Coover): 53
Lowry, Malcolm: 156–159
Lucien Leuwen (Stendhal): 76
Lucky Pierre (Coover): 62–63
Lukács, Georg: 4–5

Mack, Drew: 106
Mailer, Norman: 145
McLuhan, Marshall: 19
Major, Clarence: 24
Malamud, Bernard: 25
Mallarmé, Stéphane: 113
Malory, Thomas: 17
Mann, Thomas: 15, 113
Man Without Qualities, The (Musil): 36–37
Majorie Morningstar (Wouk): 23
Marlowe, Christopher: 2
Márquez, Gabriel Garcia: 7, 113, 153, 155–56
Marston, John: 2
Masson, David: 4
Mauriac, Claude: 15
Mayakovsky, Vladimir: 11
Meditations on Quixote (Ortega y Gasset): 151, 160
Melville, Herman: 138, 140, 143
Metamorphosis, The (Kafka): 26
Michener, James: 107
Middlemarch (Eliot): 65
Middleton, Thomas: 2
Milton, John: 3, 141
Mulata (Asturias): 155
Mulligan Stew (Sorrentino): 23
Murphy (Beckett): 26
Musil, Robert: 15, 36–37, 42, 113

Nabokov, Vladimir: 23, 71, 79, 139–40, 159
National Intelligencer: 106
Nietzsche, Friedrich: 18, 140
Nixon, Richard: 55, 58–59

"Nobody Ever Died From It" (Fiedler): 146, 147
No! In Thunder (Fiedler): 135
"Nude Croquet" (Fiedler): 146, 147

Oglesby, Carl: 35–36, 38
Olson, Charles: 140
One Hundred Years of Solitude (Márquez): 7, 113, 155–56
Onetti, Juan Carlos: 153
Origin of the Brunists, The (Coover): 46ff.
Ortega y Gasset, Jose: 151, 160

Pages from a Cold Island (Exley): 91–92
"Panel Game, The" (Coover): 55
Paracriticisms (Hassan): 14, 16
Peckham, Morse: 14
Pérec, Georges: 25
Petrarca, Francesco: 2
Picon, Gaëtan: 19
Pirandello, Luigi: 18
Plaisir du texte, Le: see *Pleasure of the Text, The*
Pleasure of the Text, The (Barthes): 16, 27, 28
Poe, Edgar Allan: 30
Poetics (Aristotle): 2–3
Political Fable, A (Coover): 62
Ponge, Francis: 13
Pontiac: 106
Portrait of the Artist as a Young Man, A (Joyce): 26, 79–80
Poulet, Georges: 14
Pound, Ezra: 14, 15, 113
Pricksongs and Descants (Coover): 46, 49, 55
Proust, Marcel: 15, 27, 65, 113
Public Burning, The (Coover): 45, 46, 52, 55, 57–62, 107
Puig, Manuel: 7
Pull Down Vanity (Fiedler): 135
Pynchon, Thomas: 23, 25

Queneau, Raymond: 15
Quijote: see *Don Quixote*

Rabelais, Francois: 15
Raglan, Lord: 105
Ragtime (Doctorow): 107
Recognitions, The (Gaddis): 145
Reed, Ishmael: 107
Reid, Alistair: 153
Rhetoric of Fiction, The (Booth): 79
Richardson, Samuel: 107, 110, 137
Rilke, Maria: 13
Rimbaud, Arthur: 11, 15
Robbe-Grillet, Alain: 13, 19
Roche, Maurice: 25
Roethke, Theodore: 104
Roots (Haley): 107

Rosenberg, Ethel: 58, 61–62
Rosenberg, Julius: 58, 61–62
Rosset, Barney: 48
Roth, Philip: 25, 103
Roussel, Raymond: 13, 15

Sade, Marquis de: 15
Sale, Roger: 88
Salmagundi: 137
Sarmiento, Domingo Faustino: 153
Sarraute, Nathalie: 13
Sayers, Dorothy: 34
Scarlet Letter, The (Hawthorne): 86
"Scene d'Amour": see "Love Scene"
Scharlatt, Hal: 60
Schlegel, August Wilhelm von: 14
Scholes, Robert: 45
Seaver, Richard: 61
Second Skin (Hawkes): 117–32
"Secret Miracle, The" (Borges): 37, 38, 43
Señor presidente, El (Asturias): 154
Shakespeare, William: 3, 120–21, 138, 141
Singer, Isaac Bashevis: 25, 143–44
Sirius (Stapledon): 142–43
62: A Model Kit (Cortázar): 155
Smith, Alexander: 152
Snow White (Barthelme): 7
Socrates: 17
Sollers, Philippe: 25
Solotaroff, Ted: 60, 61
Sontag, Susan: 9–13, 14, 17, 19
Sorel, Georges: 15
Sorrentino, Gilbert: 23
Sossi, Ron: 53
Sot-Weed Factor, The (Barth): 96, 97, 109
Spanking the Maid (Coover): 46, 63
Speak, Memory (Nabokov): 79
Stael, Madame de: 110
Stapledon, Olaf: 142–43
Starobinski, Jean: 14
Statements Two: 46
Stein, Gertrude: 13, 14, 15, 23, 26, 29, 31, 113
Stendhal (Marie Henri Beyle): 76
Sterne, Laurence: 15, 19, 113
Stevens, Wallace: 15
Still, Clyfford: 29
Stop-time (Conroy): 82–86
Styron, William: 25, 107
Sukenick, Ronald: 18, 24, 25, 27, 80, 82
Susann, Jacqueline: 140

Take It or Leave It (Federman): 27
Tanner, Tony: 79
Tasso, Torquato: 3
Tecumseh: 106
"Teeth, The" (Fiedler): 146
Tempest, The (Shakespeare): 120–21
"Theme of the Traitor and the Hero, The" (Borges): 134
Theological Position, A (Coover): 46
"Theological Position, A" (Coover): 53
Theophrastus: 5
Thomas, Dylan: 86–87
"Tlön, Uqbar, Orbis Tertius" (Borges): 154
Todorov, Tzvetan: 12
To Forget Venice (Brusati): 69
Tolstoy, Leo: 27, 146
Tathe Gentiles (Fiedler): 146
Tournier, Michel: 47
Tragic Vision, The (Krieger): 16
Tristram Shandy (Sterne): 19, 113
Trotsky, Leon: 34–35
Tzara, Tristan (Samuel Rosenstock): 15
T/Zero (Calvino): 26

Ulysses (Joyce): 3, 7, 138, 140, 147, 153
Unamuno, Miguel: 113
Under the Volcano (Lowry): 156–58
Universal Baseball Association, The (Coover): 46, 55
Updike, John: 81–82

Vidal, Gore: 23
Virgil: 103

Waiting for the End (Fiedler): 135
War and Peace (Tolstoy): 27, 146
Warhol, Andy: 13
Wellek, René: 8n.5
Wells, H. G.: 20, 139
"What Used to be Called Dead" (Fiedler): 147
"Whatever Happened to Gloomy Gus of the Chicago Bears" (Coover): 59
Whitman, Walt: 103, 109
Williams, William Carlos: 43, 103, 110
Wilson, Bob: 12
Wolfe, Tom: 36
Woolf, Virginia: 14, 15, 71, 113, 152
Wouk, Herman: 23

Yeats, William Butler: 15

NOVEL VS. FICTION

The Contemporary Reformation

Jackson Cope begins his introduction to *Novel vs. Fiction* with an extended comparison between contemporary literature and the great Renaissance "reformation" in literature in the sixteenth and seventeenth centuries. That reformation, he argues, like our contemporary one, was predicated in part on "an unmistakable symbiosis between an assertive body of critical theory, generic definition and prescription, and the enrichment writers receive from them as both validation and challenge to the enterprize of turning fantasy into new forms of fiction."

Novel vs. Fiction is a collection of essays and statements by some of the foremost critics and writers of our time that repeat and create this kind of enriching symbiosis among criticism, theory and literature.

Besides important essays by Robert Alter on John Fowles, Max Schulz on John Barth, Donald Wineke on John Hawkes, this collection offers general discussion of the contemporary reformation of the genres, contexts and geographies in traditional and innovative fictions by Jackson Cope, Geoffrey Green, Christine Brooke-Rose and Peter Bailey.

Finally, in-depth interviews with Leslie Fiedler and Robert Coover on their own and others' work and a remarkable (and *readable*) essay by Raymond Federman, "What are Experimental Novels and Why are There So Many left Unread?," round out this volume so that it offers, as a whole, important understandings and approaches to what is so often baffling in contemporary letters.